MUD WALLS
and
STEEL MILLS

Richard W. Taylor + M. M. Thomas

MUD WALLS and STEEL MILLS

God and Man at Work in India

Friendship Press • New York

Library of Congress Catalog Card Number: 63-8684

PRINTED IN THE UNITED STATES OF AMERICA

This manuscript was prepared just prior to the Chinese-Indian clashes along the border area. These clashes have produced certain changes in the thinking of the Indian people and the policies of the Indian Government, particularly with regard to nonalignment. This fact should be kept in mind as the section on Promoting Policies of Peace, pages 31-33, is read.

Contents

MUD WALLS
and
STEEL MILLS

Introduction

With political independence in 1947, India entered a period of national development. In 1949 the people gave themselves a constitution in which they committed themselves to build a nation-state to be their instrument for promoting national unity, personal freedom, and social justice. Through the execution of the first and second Five-Year Plans, India has been fighting economic poverty by striving to increase agricultural productivity, to industrialize the country, and to enhance the nation's standard of living. She has now inaugurated the third Plan, which will go a long way toward producing a self-generating economy. She is also seeking to stimulate, direct, and control changes in the structures and values of the joint family,* caste, village, and other traditional institutions of common life with a view to developing new, dynamic patterns of community.

The search for new patterns of political, economic, and social life expresses the Indian people's search for a new selfhood. It is the struggle to define anew the nature and destiny of man and society and to bring this to realization. Therefore it constitutes a real revolution not only in the means of living, but also in the meaning of life. The ferment touches traditional culture and religion in depth. To a large extent self-realization as the secular fulfillment of an historical mission is a new concept in India; but it has become the source of a renaissance of India's ancient cultures and religions.

This book is an attempt to survey this revolution which touches so deeply the totality of the life of the peoples of India, including the small Christian minority. But why should the Christian church in North America study this revolution in India and be concerned about it? Of course, the Christians and churches of India are as much involved in the ferment as other segments of Indian society, and for this reason it is in their narrow self-interest to relate themselves creatively to the new situation. Perhaps churches outside the country will have a certain interest in seeing how

* Indian terms, including "joint family" and "caste" are defined in the Appendix.

their fellow Christians in India make this adjustment, but this narrow communal fellow-feeling cannot make the concern genuinely Christian.

The church is concerned primarily with the purpose of God for mankind as revealed in Christ and with the activity of God in the history of peoples to fulfill his purpose. The assumption behind this book is that the study of current Indian politics, society, and culture can become a study in theology, a study in understanding what God is doing in India today. No doubt this assumption is astounding, but it is part of the many important rediscoveries by the ecumenical movement in recent years which Christians of this generation have begun to take seriously in their thinking about the world around them. Three of these rediscoveries may be put briefly as follows:

The redemption that Jesus Christ offers is the redemption of the world. No doubt the world refers primarily to the world of persons; but the world of persons is involved in the processes of nature, society, and history and cannot be considered or saved in isolation. Therefore, Christ's judgment and redemption is social and cosmic and includes within its scope the world of science and technology, of politics, society, and culture, of religions and secular ideologies. The Christian hope guaranteed by the Resurrection of Jesus Christ is that *all things* will be summed up in him.

The gospel of Jesus Christ is the news of the word and deed of God, which word and deed are for the world but not of it. Therefore the gospel should not be identified with any one culture, political order, social ideology, or moral system. As transcending them all, it is the divine power for their judgment and redemption. It is this understanding which gives the Church the ability to relate itself positively, but critically, to all the creative movements of the renewal of man and his world without absolutizing any of them.

Christ is present and active in the world of today, engaged in a continuous dialogue with men and nations, affirming his kingly rule over them through the power of his law and his love. The history of Christ's deeds between his resurrection and his coming again in glory holds all other histories within its context and control. So the mission of the Church is not to save itself from the revolutions of our time but, in the light of Jesus Christ, to discern in them God's creating, judging, and redeeming activity, and to witness to his kingdom waiting to manifest itself in them.

These convictions of faith perhaps raise more problems than they solve. While the history of God's deeds between Christ's resurrection and his coming again holds all other histories within its context and control, can we really understand *how* it holds them under control? To what extent can faith discern God's purpose in a particular period of history? How far does this remain masked or ambiguous? Even if Christian faith has insights about God's kingdom in the world, can they be translated into secular insights so that men of other faiths and of no faith can share them? Some of these questions we shall consider in due course. Here it is sufficient for us to know that the ways in which the people of India struggle to give expression to their new sense of dignity and historical purpose, in the structures of their personal and social existence, are part of God's dealing with them, of their Yes and No to his law and love and of his answer in judgment and mercy; and that therefore it is relevant for believers in Christ (such as North American Christian students) to study them.

The discernment of God's presence and activity in the Indian revolution can never be considered purely as an academic inquiry. It is faith seeking understanding, and its end is greater obedience in faith. Such discernment is given to the Church so that the Church's life and ministry may be an effective witness to the activity of God in that revolution. The purpose of our study is to deepen our understanding of the mission of the Church in India today. We say the mission of the Church in India, rather than the mission of the Indian church, because it is the whole world-wide Church that has its mission in every country or locality, just as much as the church in a country or locality is the manifestation of the universal reality. The Indian church can fulfill its ministry within the Indian revolution only as part of the universal fellowship of the Church. This is the justification for a study by American Christians of what is happening in India today and of what God is doing there. For them, too, this cannot be a study done in detachment, but must be the way toward a deeper involvement in obedience.

1 • TOWARD A RESPONSIBLE POLITICAL ORDER

The nationalist movement preceding independence in India took many forms, some quite violent. From the 1930's, however, following the lead of M. K. Gandhi, it centered largely on moral persuasion and nonviolent pressures including nonco-operation. Its leaders were men of exceptional ability and dedication, living simple, almost ascetic lives and spending much of their time in British jails. They were followed eagerly by all segments of India's variegated population except toward the end, when many Muslims sought an independent state of their own.

THE TRANSITION TO INDEPENDENCE

Thanks to the Gandhian leadership of the Indian national struggle for freedom and to Britain's capacity to recognize the power-realities of international relationships, the transfer of power from Britain to India took place peacefully and without breaking the ties of the British Commonwealth. This made possible a continuity with the British political tradition in India, both in institutions and in ideas. Under the leadership of Pandit Nehru it has been the endeavor of India to build the structures of a democratic nation-state that would effectively serve these five functions:

* Extend and protect the liberties of individual persons.
* Promote equality of opportunity for the development of all communities, castes, and classes and for their participation in the life of the state and society.
* Preserve and develop the unity of the nation, integrating the many traditional groups.
* Bring about economic development and raise the standard of living of the people.
* Secure a place for the nation in the international community and build relations with other nations which would facilitate national development and world peace.

These various functions are not easily reconciled. In fact, the crucial problems of Indian democracy are those that arise from the conflicts among these various goals. In several newly independent countries of Asia the demands of unity or economic development have put democratic institutions in serious jeopardy. So far, however, India has maintained a certain balance of these various functions of the state and has not wavered from her commitment to bring about social justice, national integration, and economic progress without destroying personal freedom and the possibility of open pluralism. Not that parliamentary democracy in India has become mature enough. There is still a long way to go. But India has refused to cover her immaturity by saying that democracy is not suited to the genius of India.

This does not mean that India idolizes the forms of parliamentary democracy and seeks simply to transplant them in a static way. Far from it. India realizes that parliamentary democracy must grow in the country in its own way, reshaping indigenous culture and taking roots in its soil; and that variations in its structures are necessary to make democracy work in a socially backward and economically underdeveloped country. But India has so far not sought to tamper with the essentials of parliamentary democracy. We cannot say what will happen to Indian democracy in the next decade. But barring extremists, i.e. the Communalists and the Communists, there is general recognition that the economic and social transformations which India may achieve through democratic processes will be more stable and more conducive to responsible human existence than those that may be achieved by shorter paths.

TASKS THE NATION FACES

Some tasks the Indian State confronts raise problems, as we shall see, for democratic structure.

Developing Political Democracy

Underdevelopment in this area has been recognized at two levels. On the first, the alignment of political forces and ideologies has not yet led to the emergence of a real political opposition at the national level. Freedom of organization, of press and platform, and the political debates inside and outside the state and national legislatures have given rise to numerous political parties; but none of these has yet elected the 50 members to the 600-member Lok Sabha re-required to form an officially recognized opposition. That the Congress still remains too much in the halo of the pre-independence national movement to consider itself, or to be considered by the people as a whole, as a mere party is a major factor in the situation. Nehru's leadership increases this. There is truth in the allegation that India is a one-party democracy. But considering the need for symbols of national unity, it is impossible to think that it would be advantageous to the political life of the nation as a whole if, as some social thinkers have suggested, Nehru resigned from office and the Congress were encouraged to split just to create an artificial opposition. So the only way left, then, is to preserve the conditions of freedom that can lead to the development of a real opposition.

On another level political democracy still remains an imposition from the top. The Constitution was formulated by a Constituent Assembly elected by 14 per cent of the people. Political democracy has still to be brought into meaningful relationship with the people through developing the means for their effective political education and participation. While literacy is important, it cannot be equated with education. The greater need is for organizations to educate the people for citizenship and the effective exercise of political responsibility at the local level.

The three general elections have been massive means of popular education in the exercise of the democratic franchise. But that is not enough. For this reason the idea of developing the ancient village *panchayats* in a new form has come into being. Already in several states these local units of self-government have been endowed with real power to plan and execute economic and social development projects in their neighborhoods, and act as the local units of state power. It is clear that this is a venture full of perils. If *panchayatiraj* is not to fall into the hands of people with traditional economic vested interests (such as landlords) and social prejudices (such as caste leaders), such decentralizations of power must go hand in hand with radical social change. Its efficiency also requires a crash program of education in administrative and technical skills. The major risk is that the authoritarianism and the irrationalism of India's traditional culture may erupt and revolt against democratic values altogether. Nevertheless, the proposition that nothing is real unless it is local is as true for democracy as for anything else. Indian democracy must become meaningful to the people at large or it will wither like a potted plant without manure and water. Hence there is a great deal to be said for the movement toward *panchayatiraj,* which gives to each a voice in government.

Promoting Social Justice

In India women, outcastes, tribal people, and other groups have been suffering discriminatory treatment in society for centuries. The Constituent Assembly made the practice of untouchability a penal offense and made freedom from discrimination on the basis of religion, caste, race, or sex a fundamental law of the land. Legislative enactments have recodified the Hindu law and have written equality of men and women in marriage, divorce, inheritance, and adoption into the statute book.

These are important expressions of the democratic doctrine of equality under the law. But some of these traditional groups are so backward that it is impossible for them to compete with the rest on an equal footing. What they need is not merely freedom from discrimination, but protective discrimination so that they can be specially cared for until they can stand on their own with the rest. Such protective discrimination has been provisionally given to the scheduled castes, scheduled tribes, and similar backward communities. In one sense such discrimination in the name of social justice is an extension of the rule of law, but several dangers are inherent in it. While protective discrimination is given provisionally, when the initial inequality is overcome there is likelihood of its becoming a new vested interest. Then the protective discrimination in the name of social justice becomes antithetic to the rule of law. Secondly, since the rights given by way of protective discrimination are given not to individuals but to traditional groups, it may enhance the communal tendencies in the body politic and prevent the emergence of individuality among the people. Also in this connection, there are some who fear that dependence on protective discrimination will lead to over-dependence on politicians for continued special favors in return for block votes, instead of the encouragement of individual and group initiative in the surmounting of handicaps. Already it is accepted party policy to include candidates from the backward groups in a balanced slate. This often also involves continuing favors for these groups.

Social justice has been broadly defined in India as the building up of material, social, and moral conditions conducive to the personal development and social welfare of the people. No doubt in the past it was the traditional community (the joint family, caste, and village institutions) that provided for the people the conditions of welfare as the traditional society understood it. But today these are in various degrees of disintegration. The Constitution, in its Directive Principles of State Policy, invests the state as the organ of the whole national community with the responsibility of seeing to the provision of free compulsory education for all children up to the age of fourteen, of care for the handicapped, of a better level of nutrition, housing, and standard of living for all people, and of work, a living wage, and the full enjoyment of leisure and social and cultural opportunities to all. In this sense the political ideal accepted in India is that of the welfare state. The Community Development Projects constitute a massive program for implementing this ideal.

In a country like India, with traditional communities unable to conceive of welfare in a broad and dynamic way or to meet its demands, the new national community and its instrument, the state, must take a very heavy responsibility in building the conditions of social welfare. This is, however, different from a state monopoly of welfare activities. In a democracy, while the state provides the legal framework and the material resources and exercises a good deal of control in the interest of the common good, the goal of the state is to stimulate self-help projects by voluntary societies and by neighborhood communities.

The Indian state is most clear about this. For instance, the aim of the Community Projects is precisely to make the village society capable of organizing itself to help itself through *panchayats* and co-operative efforts. However, the danger of state invasion of the total area of social life is not altogether imaginary in a situation where the voluntary organizations for social work and activity are few and weak. For this reason, one welcomes the emphasis in the Sarvodaya movement on community action *(Lokniti* and *Janasakti)* as the levers of social welfare. Christian churches and Christian social agencies have a great part to play in stimulating voluntary activities for the welfare of the people.

Strengthening National Unity

Independence brought a sense of selfhood to the nation which found expression in the nation-state, but it also made all the traditional groups within the nation self-conscious. Western friends tend to think of India and other Asian and

African countries as ultranationalistic, but as time goes on we find that, after the days of the national struggle for freedom, nationalism loses its strength and dynamism and is threatened by the divisiveness of religious, tribal, caste, linguistic, and regional factionalism. The revival of old indigenous traditions, sometimes in initial support of nationalism, has in a sense enhanced the strength of sectarian fanaticism, because the old memories are of isolation and segregation or of domination, exploitation, and mutual conflicts. Frankly, it was only during the British period, thanks to British power, common education in a common language that happened to be English, and the Indian national movement, that a sense of common nationhood emerged.

Today the symbols of nationhood seem less emotionally appealing than the traditional memories which separate. Adult franchise, at least in the short run, has strengthened groupism, for leaders have to get the votes of the masses whose loyalties are primarily to their caste, linguistic, and regional groups. Politically such groupism is not unlike the getting out of the "Catholic vote" or the "Negro vote" for particular candidates and propositions in America. In India such appeals to caste, lingustic and regional groups, and their internal loyalties tend to emphasize their differentness from other groups and to give the group appealed to, as well as to the groups they are thus differentiated from, an increasingly strong group consciousness. One aspect of this is the increase of social pressures in many regions against the hiring of "outsiders"—from other regions—for any government jobs, even on the basis of merit. There are similar pressures from within the churches to regionalize employment by Christian institutions, such as schools and hospitals. At election times there are also efforts to line up the vote of the "Christian community" for particular parties and candidates.

In India the first threat to national unity came from religious communalism, which with partition led to Hindu-Muslim riots. The ideal of the secular state, with its separation of the state from all religious establishments and with a state guarantee of religious freedom, had gone a long way toward preventing the development of religious communalism in politics. But with the strengthening of the Jan Sangh (the Hindu communal political party), the emergence once more of the Muslim League into the limelight as a political party of Muslims, and the revival of the Kashmir issue by Pakistan, communalism is again having a new lease on life. The specter of communalism is raised in several ways by the Kashmir issue. The man in the street feels uneasy about the loyalties of his Muslim neighbors. The most responsible members of government fear that any kind of "plebiscite" in Kashmir would lead to the systematic fanning of religious-group feeling by interested parties and that this could only lead to the kind of appalling bloodshed that so surprised and shocked them at the time of the partition of India.

The secular state and secular democratic political parties still remain the primary foundation of India's hope in bringing about a sense of nationhood transcending religious differences. When the Constitution was being formulated, the

Christian community was the first to renounce all special political safeguards and status as a political minority. In fact, the guarantee of freedom of religious propagation as a fundamental right of every man was a generous gesture in response to this stand of the Christians. Christians have on the whole continued to strengthen the secularism of politics and the state. They can do no small service to national unity by continuing to do so. Such action is also necessary to prevent the Christian community itself from becoming a caste-like, static, closed society, which would be to forget its mission to all the people of India.

A more serious threat to unity came with the linguistically based reorganization of the states of India in 1958, when the boundaries of the various states of India were redrawn largely on the basis of grouping together, in one state, people speaking the same language. While it was a good idea to bring the government nearer to the people in their own regional language, this produced linguistic and regional fanaticism that knew no bounds. In the days of the national independence movement, education and politics were the two sources of national unity. With the new emphasis on regional language as opposed to English, and the emergence of regional lobbies in politics, education and politics now tend to become threats to national integration. Those enthusiasts who wanted immediately to adopt Hindi as the only official language, and the Pure Tamil fanatics who sought separation of Tamilnad or Dravidastan from the Indian Union, had tremendous appeal to the people in their regions. Fortunately, all parties have now come to realize the danger inherent in a free play of fanaticism, and several all-India consultations on national integration have helped to stem the tide of fissiparous forces, for the moment at any rate. The renewed emphasis on English in education is also welcome in this connection.

A more pervasive threat to national integration is, of course, the impact of caste communalism or caste consciousness on Indian politics. Communal or group exclusiveness is written into the very heart of the traditional caste system. For this reason, even when caste has ceased to perform its traditional functions it becomes the emotional focus of group solidarity in the organized fight for political power and economic advantage. Political democracy and economic development have resulted in giving a heightened importance to caste structures. Sociological studies of politics in some states of India have shown quite clearly that the fact of caste determines in large part the political behavior even of members of national political parties. For instance, in a village one party may be formed on the base of the upper-caste, traditional elite and another on the former outcastes. These will reach downward and upward in the traditional caste structure, across formerly uncrossable caste lines, just far enough to garner enough votes to win elections locally. Much of the electioneering will be on the basis of appeals to caste loyalties, or rather will involve calling for the defeat of the still despised other castes. Another party may be formed of the artisan castes in the middle of the social structure. Different national parties may be identified with different caste-based groups in different villages and in different regions. The same sort of thing happens in the political exploitation of caste structures in the cities.

Recently a committee of the Congress Party considered the question of whether laws can be promulgated at least to prevent the outbursts of sectarian fanaticism from leading to riots. For instance, is it possible to make the organization of communal parties illegal? Is it possible to amend the penal law so that not only individuals but groups or communities responsible for intergroup clashes can be prosecuted and punished? Can the Preventive Detention Act (used widely during the British period and since) be used against political leaders engaged in fomenting intergroup tensions? All these checks would have far-reaching implications for the democratic system, but they cannot be ruled out. It is important to foster legal checks and preserve a balance of group loyalties and to be firm in dealing with disturbances that create disorder if a democratic structure ensuring fundamental rights is to be developed. It is far better to adopt temporary measures of expediency, with safeguards against their misuse and with provision for return to normality built into them, rather than to be forced into a situation where the nation has to choose between political democracy or national unity.

In the long run, however, unity depends on the common recognition by the various Indian groups of the essentially composite character of Indian nationhood, and on the efforts to build mutual confidence among majority and minority groups. If democratic unity is the goal, the slogan "one religion, one culture, one language" as the basis of nationality at either the state or national level is dangerous. It does not matter whether it comes from the majority groups who want to dominate the rest or from the minority groups who want to separate from the rest. Besides, this is a slogan that looks backward and not forward, and which denies the fact that in India nationhood is something that is only in process of coming into being. That is why measures are now needed to create mutual confidence among the various groups that compose the nation. To foster such confidence the Government of India has rightly created special offices like those of the Commissioner for Scheduled Castes and Tribes and the Commissioner for Linguistic Minorities. More such organs of state may be needed. They can be responsive to the legitimate grievances of groups who feel their essential rights threatened. But mutual confidence cannot rest solely on what the state does. It rests on toleration of each other, the development of a community of values, and the effort of all groups together to build the nation. At this level, Christians have certain special contributions to make. In their faith that mankind has a common destiny in Christ they have a resource to strengthen the idea of common human solidarity. This can break down isolationism and lead to mutual forgiveness and acceptance.

Achieving Economic Development

More will be said about this in the next chapter. Here we touch mainly on the tensions that the achievement of this goal creates with respect to other goals.

Can India achieve rapid economic progress without destroying the essentials of parliamentary democracy? No political question is more important than this one. India's is a unique experiment. European countries as well as Japan achieved industrialization first and extended democratic rights to the people afterwards. In America there were neither feudal interests nor an entrenched static social structure to fight against. Unlike the situation in the West, the original stimulus for development in India came as a result of the impact of alien, developed economies and did not rise from an inner transformation. India enters the field of economic development rather late in the day.

In this context the accumulation of capital, stimulation of enterprise, training in technical skills, building the agricultural base, and transformation of society and culture, all of which are necessary for economic development, raise tremendous problems. Looking at things pragmatically, without ideologically colored glasses, it is clear to even the most conservative economists that in the underdeveloped economies of Asia the state must play a large role in accumulating the resources and creating the conditions necessary for development, and to make economic plans and supervise their implementation. The question India faces, however, is whether this role can be exercised effectively under a parliamentary system, which requires that, for the changes, sacrifice, and disciplines needed, popular consent be obtained from a people already living at starvation level.

India's first, second, and third Five-Year Plans have shown that planning and freedom need not be considered totally antithetical and that democratic planning for development of the national economy is certainly possible, within limits.

The threats to the idea of democratic planning for development come from two sides. One comes from the side of the advocates of totalitarian or authoritarian planning. They believe that development will not reach the self-generating stage unless coercive processes are used much more than is possible in a political democracy. From the other side there is a threat from those committed to the ideology of laissez-faire capitalism. They feel that any kind of state planning or control of economic life is destructive to political democracy. There is some truth in each of these arguments, but taken in toto they are mistaken and even dangerous. It is the conviction of the people of India that *both* democracy *and* planning for development can go together and that it is much better for democracy in an underdeveloped country like India to follow the path of a mixture of individual, state, and co-operative enterprises, under the general supervision of the state as the only organ of national community, rather than to let economic power become the monopoly of either the state or of private enterprise. It is only dogmatists of laissez-faire who will question this approach, and then only if they are blind to pragmatic realities of the Indian situation. In fact, some of them seem unable to recognize the fact that even in the American economy the state plays no small role.

The transformation of agriculture along scientific lines is priority number one for the nation's industrial development, regardless of whether this is to be in laissez-faire or mixed economy. This, however, is closely linked with the changes in traditional social structure (joint family, caste, and village) and traditional agrarian relations (involving land tenure and a feudal type of economy) which have been major integrating factors in society. Land reforms in the form of abolition of *zamindari,* tenancy legislation, ceiling on holdings, regulation of rent, and rehabilitation of the landless have moved in the right direction. But the results are not yet satisfactory. More radical changes are called for in the traditional socio-economic life in the rural sector.

It is in this connection that the idea of co-operative farming has been proposed. Here Indian democracy is faced with two perils, both of which have to be avoided. On the one hand, if democracy is not able to create the agrarian conditions necessary for industrialization, it may lead the people already involved in a revolution of rising economic expectations to reject democracy and follow other paths for quicker progress. On the other hand, agrarian reform must not create so much disintegration and demoralization as to destroy the moral and political stability required for democracy. But it is no use exaggerating one peril or the other. The need is to see both and to steer a course which helps and does not hinder political democracy. To many, co-operative farming is that middle course. Besides, it seems to be the only course which can give the large number of landless wage earners some place and significance in the economic and social structure. Christians in many parts of the country belong to the landless groups. Their contribution to the nation will no doubt be more significant if co-operative farming comes to be adopted, especially if they are trained for significant participation in the co-operative movement.

Promoting Policies of Peace

India has been obliged to shape its international policy in a world situation dominated by the struggle between the Western and Soviet military blocs. India's policy of non-alignment with military blocs has led many in America to misunderstand India's position as one of neutrality in the moral struggle between democracy and communism in the world. The fact is that it is India's political commitment to democracy that has led to her uncommitted stand in relation to the military blocs. The "immorality of neutrality" equation is valid only if the first line of democracy's defense against communism in Asia in general and India in particular is the military one. This is clearly not so. Communism's first line of attack, in Asia at any rate, is internal and not external; it comes out of the deep-seated conviction among the socially depressed groups seeking social justice, the economically poor fighting poverty, and the idealist intelligentsia searching for a path of effective service to the nation, that what they seek cannot be had through democracy. Therefore the first line of defense is social reconstruction. The reliance on the military may in fact hide this truth and make communism all the more a threat. Further, the experience of Asian countries in the Western blocs shows that Western power has in fact frequently been supporting reactionary parties in power against the legitimate aspirations of the people, who for this reason have been more easily drawn to the communist camp. In fact, India's military nonalignment has been dictated precisely by her commitment to political democracy.

It is quite possible to argue that in India itself many have confused military neutrality with political neutrality, that Indian leaders have minimized the communist threat to democracy arising from Soviet military power and that India's policy has shown a moralistic approach which has not revealed her appreciation of the moral dilemmas of power in the modern world. True in part as these suggestions may be, on the whole India's foreign policy cannot but be interpreted except as a reflection of her commitment to the development of democratic society within India and throughout the world.

That the policy of nonalignment has helped to develop a psychological area of peace in the world as a whole seems beyond doubt. For this reason, India has come to represent the concern for peace of the peoples of the world. Reaction against India's military action in Goa seems to have been due in part to the idea that India is committed to some sort of pacifism. This is not true; no modern nation can be pacifist. Nevertheless, India's service as a symbol for world peace has helped to place her on the political map of the world in a way nothing else could have done. After all, peace is the essential condition for India's own development. Any major war would make her development plans impossible through lack of funds, if in no other way. The policy of nonalignment has helped India avoid the danger of the internal political scene being dominated by the struggle between the extreme ideological Right and Left. This has led to a certain broad unity among the political forces in the country and has contributed in no small way to the healthy development of the body politic.

In spite of occasional outbursts of irritation against Indian neutralism, many leaders of both West and East have come to recognize the sincere concern for national development and world peace underlying India's nonalignment. This, coupled with the desire of both West and East to have India "on their side" as far as possible, has led to massive aid to India to implement her plans of economic development. So in all these areas India's national interest has been well served by her foreign policy. Leaving aside India's contribution to world peace, looking at things either from the point of view of political democracy or the interest of national development, India's foreign policy must be evaluated as a success.

There are no doubt many unsolved problems, especially those involving relations with Pakistan and China. Probably they show the limitations or failures of India's policy. But it is very difficult to see that any other policy could have done better to solve these problems. There are other crucial tasks and problems as well. We have touched only some of those that vitally relate to the nation's task in preserving and developing a democratic order.

2 • ECONOMIC DEVELOPMENT

Poverty haunts all the hopes of India today. Squalor, malnutrition, and unemployment or underemployment are too common to require documentation. Stories about the great wealth and luxury of a few rajas, ex-rulers of princely states, give a misleading economic picture of India. It is true that, relative to the general population, the rich are very rich indeed. However, they no longer have the income from most of their hereditary lands nor from the taxes that they once collected. They are themselves taxed heavily both on income and on wealth. In many cases much of their remaining capital is invested in new enterprises. But the poor are the dominant economic fact of Indian society. In terms of ordinary American experience they are as unimaginably poor as the few rajas are undreamably rich. This poverty is most apparent among the masses in the prevalence of semi-starvation, lack of adequate protection against the rain, the cold, and the heat in regard both to housing and clothing, and a very high rate of sickness and disease. This has led to a high death rate, which has declined dramatically as modern medicine and drugs have found their way into more and more sections of cities and villages. Even this has not been an unmixed blessing, since mouths have tended to multiply more rapidly than food.

The normal daily wage for an unskilled laborer is about forty-four cents. Almost all laborers belong to this category. The normal daily wage for a woman is less. About one quarter of the labor force (most of which is agricultural) does not really have *any* work, and few indeed are regularly employed throughout the year. Economic progress, therefore, is that without which neither political development nor social progress can take place.

Without economic development, democratic development will be completely blocked. As we have said, India is the first country in the world to make a major effort to achieve a modern industrial economy through democratic planning under a parliamentary government. Laissez-faire capitalism may theoretically be out of the question for India for the very same reasons that it is no longer actually practiced in America. Actually, however, this question does not arise for India, since there would not be enough private capital even to begin to develop adequately the basic necessities in industry, agriculture, and natural resources. Moreover, cultural and social conditions for such development are far from ideal. One reason is that a considerable segment of large private industry is now under the control of a former subcaste of big money-lenders and traders, who are united to each other by their old subcaste loyalties. In their eagerness for large and quick returns on their investments, they have earned the reputation of being unscrupulous in their exploitation of the public, their employees, other businessmen, their own firms, and corruptible government officers.

India has chosen democratic planning in a mixed economy with some of the means of production in private hands and some in the hands of various public corporations. In structure this mixed economy is not so very different from those of Great Britain and some Scandinavian countries, but these countries did not adopt such structures until long after their own industrial revolutions.

INDUSTRIAL DEVELOPMENT AND THE FIVE-YEAR PLANS

India is now in the period of the Third Five-Year Plan, which runs into 1966. Yet this is only the second five-year period of planned intensive economic development. The First Plan was preparatory rather than developmental in nature. While laying the groundwork for the future it sought to rehabilitate the economy, which was damaged first by the war and then by the partition of India and Pakistan at the time of independence. Its emphasis was on agriculture and communications in order to prepare the economy to take a step towards industrialization and to accelerate capital formation during later plans.

The Community Development Program is a major item carried over from the First Plan. We describe it in the next chapter as a kind of intensive agricultural extension program. With considerable technical aid from Americans experienced in the training of county agents, rural home economists, and others, this program has spread widely. By the end of 1959 it was reported to include over 300,000 villages, representing a population of more than 161 million.

Another major carry-over from the First Plan is to be found in the huge multipurpose development schemes centered around irrigation and power at Bhakra Nangal, the Damodar Valley, and elsewhere, which were begun during that period. All of these depend heavily for inspiration and somewhat for technical matters on the pioneering Tennessee Valley Authority. Even to those critics of the TVA who claim that private power companies could have and would have carried out that project to at least equal advantage, it must be clear that there are no private companies with enough capital to do this in India today.

Under the Railway Board, the consolidation and expansion of government railways, which are the backbone of communications in India, has been a remarkably sound venture. Starting at independence with the largest railway system in Asia, this board has earned repeated commendation from experts of the World Bank and other economists as an excellent risk for many and increasing loans of various types in its program of expansion and modernization.

The industrial achievements in the Second Plan period were truly remarkable. These centered in heavy metallurgical and chemical industries. Perhaps typical is the pattern of the basic steel industry. Three huge complexes have been created where there was nothing before. The capacity of each will be about one million tons. At the end of the plan period, their combined production was around two million tons and they continue to expand. These are run by government corporations. The complex at Rourkela was built largely with West German technical aid and considerable financial aid from Germany. That at Bhilai is the showpiece of Russian aid to India. In Durgapur the plants have been planned and built by a British consortium. Equivalent modernization and expansion has taken place in the privately owned portion of the steel industry, particularly in the original steel mill in India, that of the Tata firm, the production of which has been multiplied on the basis of commercial loans and technical assistance from Kaiser Engineering.

The steel industry shows several rather typical aspects of Indian economic development. Although doctrinaire democratic socialism, even of the British variety, would suggest total nationalization of so basic an industry as steel, India has instead permitted the private sector to expand considerably, indeed perhaps about as fast as commercial credit was available. In the basic oil industry, private capital was available; therefore the major expansion has taken place in the private sector. This expansion has been comparable to that in the public sector of the steel industry, under state management.

The steel pattern also demonstrates a basic idea of current Indian planning of a mixed economy: namely, allowing for some competition in every major segment of the economy. This provides a check on how the management and efficiency of the government corporations measure up to those in the private sector of the same segment, and at the same time it makes monopolies impossible.

The progress to date would not have been possible without massive economic aid from abroad. This has been needed both absolutely and for much of the foreign exchange required to buy basic equipment and technical assistance from overseas. Reliance on foreign aid makes planning doubly difficult, since the aid available is apt to fluctuate owing to changes in national and international political situations. For the first two years of the Third Plan, however, the "Aid India Consortium" countries, which provide most of the foreign aid (these are the United States, Britain, Canada, France, West Germany, and Japan; in addition, Austria, Holland, Belgium, and Italy have recently come into the group) have undertaken to provide about $2,286,000,000. The total expenditure for public investment under the Plan in these years is expected to be about $8,645,000,000.

The Third Plan is a continuation of the Second. The emphasis is again on heavy capital goods industries as against consumer industries, since this is believed to be necessary to enable India to achieve industrialization and the real economic independence required for underwriting all other aspects of freedom. Broadly, the plan involves a total investment equivalent to about $21,613,000,000. The broad aims of this Plan include: self-sufficiency in food grains and a general increase in agricultural production to meet the needs of industry and provide for exports; expansion of basic industries like steel, fuel, and power and the establishment of machine-building capacity so that the requirements of further industrialization can be met within ten years or so; utilization to the fullest extent possible of the manpower resources of the country and ensuring a substantial expansion of employment opportunities; and, finally, a reduction of inequalities in income and wealth and a more even distribution of economic power.

AGRICULTURAL DEVELOPMENT

India has not yet reached her goal of economic freedom. So far in her progress, however, several possible roadblocks have been identified. These are now being dealt with. One of these might be identified as agriculture and agrarian relations. The production of food was very successful during the First Plan, largely due to a lengthy and unusual period of favorable weather in almost all parts of the country. Because of this success food production was not given the highest priority in the Second Plan and India is not yet self-sufficient in grain. The agricultural side of the Community Development Program has increased food production, but not enough. This has gone more slowly than had been anticipated, largely because of the traditional conservatism of farmers toward change of any kind.

On the other hand, at the time of independence there was a pressing problem of landless peasants, which was coupled with a feudal system of large land holdings. The dedication of the newly free Indian Government to the uplift of all the people gave to phased land reform a place of priority in the program similar to that in the postwar democratization of Japan under American guidance. But this too has gone slowly.

At the annual convention of the Congress Party in Nagpur in 1959, co-operative joint farming was accepted as the pattern for getting on toward a solution of these problems. It is hoped that it will both continue land reforms and break up enough of the ancient village patterns of traditionalism so as to lead farmers to accept more readily the improved methods for obtaining larger yields. Traditionalism in social patterns seems to reinforce traditionalism in agricultural patterns in many general ways. For instance, traditional dietary regulations limit the potential consumption of new crops. Another example is the traditional custom in many villages that denies to a farmer's unmarried daughters the right to go very far from home. Since one of the daughters' customary functions is the conservation of cow dung, this traditional social pattern has radically limited the improvement of compost methods. For it has meant that the girls and young women could not stray to the edge of the village where modern compost pits might best be constructed. Traditionally dung is dried in the vicinity of the house, in thin layers in the sun. Treated in this way, it does not have much potency as a fertilizer.

It is also expected that co-operative joint farming will facilitate some of those agricultural techniques that are hardly practical on the very small, fragmented land holdings presently being farmed.

Joint farming is not the collectivized farming of communism. In redistribution, ceilings are to be placed on land holdings, as has already been done in some states, and loans will be made available to co-operatives of the landless for the purchase of surplus land. Farmers will enter the farming co-operative of their own choice and will be free to withdraw. They will retain title to their land. Income will be based on their share of the land and also on their share of the labor. The income of the landless laborer in the co-operative will be based on his contributed labor.

So far the stage of actual co-operative farming has not been reached. Instead there has been a vast increase in the number of farm-oriented co-operatives for providing services for farmers that they cannot afford individually. These include co-operatives to market the farmers' produce and to encourage the production of marketable things, co-operatives to supply improved seeds, fertilizers, insecticides, and advice about their use, co-operatives to buy and hold farm machinery and dairy equipment in common, co-operatives to cope with common problems of water supply, and co-operatives to lend money for the improvement of farms. Probably these service co-operatives will be the major step at present until the farmers become familiar with their operation and confident in participating in them.

Its potential economic success aside, co-operative farming

has, like the earlier Congress adoption of the goal of a Socialist Pattern for society in 1955, proved to be an astute political move in taking potential initiative away from parties of the far Left. Now if the scheme is successful Congress gets the credit, while even if it is unsuccessful it is no longer a lively platform for political agitation.

POPULATION AND ECONOMICS

Another major economic roadblock is the problem of an expanding population. This is hardly an "explosion." Indeed, the present Indian birth rate is not appreciably higher than the American. What has happened is that the benefits from the partial availability of modern medicine have made it possible for many more to live reasonably long lives, although the average life expectancy (now 42 years for the young male) is still appallingly short by American expectations. This problem of population will be accentuated in the immediate future by the continued spread of the benefits of medicine and by the coming of age of a teen-age group that at present forms a disproportionately large percentage of the total population.

The primary economic factor is that much of the expanding national product must be used for the expanding population rather than in improving the lot of individuals or in reinvestment in further expansion. There are at least two reasons why this factor has been fully faced only recently. The first is that its magnitude was underestimated both by the Census Organization and by the Planning Commission. The corrected figures of the 1961 Census Report indicate a population of 439 million. Even the Planning Commission's projection called for only 431 million. The second reason is that a realistic resort to family planning was for long frustrated by the Gandhian contention that continence and moral fortitude formed the only proper basis for family planning and limitation. This position was reiterated by some politicians directly responsible for the government program as late as 1955.

Of course, it is possible for family limitation to take place without the use of complex mechanical or chemical aids. The middle classes of France and Britain, to take only two examples, achieved this several generations ago. Middle-class values, however, are not widely enough accepted throughout India to make this factor very important.

Within the years since this problem has been taken seriously, great strides have been made in research, education, and aid at the local level for family planning and limitation. If within the same period of time this complex of programs is as successful as, say, the program for steel productivity has been since government gave it high priority, then there appears to be at least some hope of overcoming the population roadblock to economic development.

At present, in addition to education and promulgation of various contraceptive techniques, voluntary sterilization of either male or female partners with adequate healthy living families is being advocated. This is becoming increasingly popular, especially among middle-class couples. While many in the groups of Christian doctors and intellectuals who have met to discuss these problems were at first appalled by the advocacy of sterilization, it is clear that consensus now favors it as a possibility with adequate education and safeguards.

INFLATION AND UNEMPLOYMENT

Periodically in India since before the end of the last war, inflation has been an important threat to the common man. This has been true again in recent years. At the beginning of the Second Plan the stability of price levels did not seem to be an important matter for consideration. However, within that five-year period prices went up by 20 per cent, and the tendency has not yet been checked. Such a degree of inflation adds greatly to the economic burden of all. This is especially true of unplanned inflation, which does not even serve well the possible function of being an equivalent of indirect taxation.

With the increasing population, and due to the fact that the basic industries with highest priorities in the early plans have relatively small employment potentials, unemployment stalks through all levels of society. In the predominant segment of the employable force—agricultural workers—this often takes the form of underemployment, with the traditional work which one or two men could do spread out through much of their immediate family or even through their larger family. Among day laborers in the construction and related industries, underemployment often means that any individual may work for only half of the available workdays, or even fewer.

Unemployment means no work at all. The thought of

unemployment is not comfortable for any but it seems especially to be a specter in the life of almost every college student. One of his primary reasons for studying is to prepare himself for a job. But students begin to feel quite cynical about getting jobs on the basis of ability alone. There are so many qualified applicants for each vacancy that they come to feel that only influence really pays off in getting jobs. In fact, many are not able to get jobs for a year or so after graduation, and even then these may be jobs that could be done without a college education. Recently there were over fifteen hundred qualified applicants for employment for a group of about thirty clerical jobs. Similar conditions tend to prevail for those who have gone on to postgraduate degrees or who have studied abroad. Several years ago a special civil service examination was held to recruit young but experienced men into the Indian Administrative Service, which supplies most of the top civil servants throughout India. Younger college teachers and other employed men in their age and income bracket could apply. There were tens of thousands of applications for only a few hundred positions. All of this creates a sizable segment of the population who are educated but unemployed or radically dissatisfied with their employment, and this could easily become a political tinderbox.

Of course, this unemployment exists in an economy that uses more manual labor than machines for every product and procedure. If banking or farming were to be done in India with the help of machines on such a scale as applies in America, probably more than 90 per cent of the bank clerks and of the employed farm workers would be put out of their present jobs.

Cottage industries have been encouraged under the development plans precisely because they depend very largely on human labor rather than on machines and so provide more employment, especially outside of the cities where it is most needed. These cottage industries also have been encouraged because they produce consumer goods, which the plans in these early stages have had to neglect. Many Gandhians and others also feel that these cottage industries are an essential part of Indian traditional society and as such should be used as centers for the renewal of society in economically self-sufficient villages, but this position no longer seems to be gaining headway.

THE RATE OF ECONOMIC PROGRESS

Economic progress in India has been astonishing in its rapidity. The most modern steel plants have risen where only a few years ago the basic village economy, which still persists in part in many villages, was not even a market economy of the barter form—to say nothing of a monetary economy. Rather, it was an organic economy of a kind that in the north has been called the Jajmani system. Under it, members of occupation castes gave their secular and prescribed ritual services to hereditary patrons of other castes, in return for traditional gifts of food and equipment on seasonal holy days and at the time of the observance of certain rites of passage by members of the family. This system was first thoroughly studied by a missionary social scientist less than forty years ago. The transition to social planning of multipurpose valley authorities and steel mills, to say nothing of a peaceful atomic energy enterprise, is breathtaking. Of course, the background for this among the elite has been laid by several generations of modern education and the formulation and acceptance of new values. It may also be several generations from now before the village farmer is fully able to accept all these innovations.

3 • COMMUNITY: ITS VALUES AND PATTERNS

The changing patterns of social living that have been pointed out in many recent commentaries on India are of great importance in themselves. Perhaps they are even more important for the changes in values they reflect. These underlying value changes are more basic than changes in pattern because their outcome will determine, at least in part and for the time being, just how possible it will be for individuals and groups to move toward the living of truly human lives. Some of the changing patterns and values in marriage and family life provide an example from the heart of society. Similar examples could be given from other facets of social life.

FAMILY AND MARRIAGE

Traditionally, marriages have been arranged between families, possible partners have been limited by subcaste, both arrangement and consummation have taken place at a fairly young age, and living has been in the parents' home in a joint family with common hearth and often common occupation, with all important decisions being made by the elders. The larger family, with its roots in a subcaste that limits one's possible marriage partners and even one's smoking and dining partners, defined quite fully one's way of life and provided much by way of emotional, economic, and even religious security. The deeply ingrained emotional barriers with which the larger family surrounded itself are seen most dramatically in the institution of untouchability.

A clue to the magnitude of these barriers may be found in the history of the modern missionary movement, at the point when many diligent seekers from higher castes found it impossible to *hear* the gospel that might lead to their conversion, because on the one hand acceptance of it would exclude them from their family, the seat of all of their many kinds of social security and self-identification; and on the other it would require them to partake of that most holy of meals, the Eucharist, along with persons whose presence with them during a meal had become unthinkable. Even common interdining is often still revolting to those who in maturity find rational grounds for disapproving of the social behavior involved in restricting it. The descendants of those who did receive the gospel sometimes still find it impossible to sanction marriage of their children with others in their denomination who are of different group descent.

While the ideal type of the joint family pattern of living was probably never even approximated by more than half of the families in India, it did incorporate values and serve as a focus for other values that were accepted by almost all Indians.

This joint family pattern is breaking down through the impact of many forces. Almost all of these forces are related to monetization, industrialization, urbanization, and the differing kinds of values that their acceptance tends to imply.

These forces impinge upon the family in many ways. With monetization the sons of a family and their wives, even if all remain in some common occupation, have a quite precise idea of the cash value of their contribution to the common economy. Then it seems easy to separate this out for their separate support. However, with the availability of and desire for education, increasingly it is probable that brothers will prepare for different kinds of trades, occupations, and professions and will find different kinds of jobs. This will mean that they have much less in common among themselves. Perhaps one becomes a government clerk, another a successful small business man, a third a professional government officer as a doctor, lawyer, administrator, or soldier, and a fourth stays in the village to care for the family property and to follow the traditional family occupation of goldsmithing. The boys' different educations and occupations will mean that increasingly they have less in common with their brothers and more in common with their mates in school and on the job. And differences will often be even greater between the sons and their parents.

These things alone would make traditional joint family living difficult. The fact that some of their jobs would involve frequent changes in residence at the pleasure of their private or governmental employer, so that all the brothers might be living in different towns, means that the exact style of joint family living becomes physically impossible even though the emotional ties and certain financial ties may be kept up.

Other factors also follow, especially on the distaff side. If a young man's future economic and social status can no longer be accurately predicted on the basis of his family's position, then responsible fathers will not arrange marriages for their daughters until the young men have finished their education and found jobs. This means that merely on account of their increased age brides will fit less smoothly into the ways of their husbands' families and under the domination of their mothers-in-law. That the brides will usually have spent much of this extra time getting more education themselves only deepens the gap between themselves and their parents-in-law, as well as that between themselves and their sisters-in-law.

These forces create situations favoring certain *types* of values rather than specific values, the choice of which initially seems to be somewhat open. There are, in addition, some rather specific values which seem to be coming to the fore. These include freedom for self-development and expression (this emphasis upon individual selfhood is not unrelated to the search for national selfhood), and freedom for individualized choice and valuation, including being valued by others on an individual basis.

In marriage this often means trying to give one's young children freedom to learn how to make increasingly important decisions for themselves—decisions of a sort that were largely made even for young parents by family elders. The importance of mutual love, trust, and co-operation within the family and between the husband and wife is increasingly stressed in this connection.

Radically this takes the form—in films, novels, and student discussions—of a desire for "love marriage," as a popular current film is titled, for "love rather than just a legalized husband" as student letters to the editor have sometimes put it. Enlightened sexual relations are often an important part of what is being valued here, but rather more important is a yearning for wider possibilities of mutual freedom and self-realization.

The difficulties of achieving such goals on the basis of human hope and good will appear overwhelming. In America few enough of one's friends and former classmates have really made a go of this kind of romantic marriage, working hard to avoid its many known pitfalls. But *they* have had the advantage of living according to the prevailing pattern, with the experience of their own childhood family and the observed and shared experience of their brothers, sisters, uncles, aunts, and friends to build upon. In India their counterparts operate in this area at best in a vacuum of experience and at worst with guilt born of family disapproval as well.

Few who accept the value of the love marriage as portrayed in mass media realize how unique in history and radically at one end of the spectrum of possibilities the husband-wife-minor children romantic love-based family is. It is almost the complete opposite of the radical joint family. In addition to the problem of inexperience, the very intensity of relationships and dependence among all members of the small family group appears to provide a context where the full personal development (the most widely sought new value in this area) of children and adults may be truncated.

At present even fully arranged marriages may incorporate some of the new values. Such a marriage between, say, a young physician and a girl who has almost finished college, who have not met before the formal announcement of their coming marriage, may shock the girl's classmates who will be permitted to finish college before marrying someone whom they have at least met and approved. However, as this young couple begin to live together, perhaps in the same building or town as the boy's parents, they begin to share a sexual, social, intellectual, and family life together that just because of the frequent influence on it of, and support from, relatives may really make it more possible for their selfhood and that of their children to develop than would be the case in a radical renunciation of even modified traditional patterns and their replacement by patterns that have become attached to these values elsewhere.

In addition to the forces impinging on family patterns from changing social structure and from new value judgments about love and self-realization in marriage, more general new value judgments have been codified in legislation dealing primarily with divorce, inheritance, and adoption. Recently an act was passed forbidding the dowry system (the bridegroom price), which is found throughout India. Among Christians it is particularly rigid in some parts of South India and is deeply entrenched among the ancient Syrian Christians, for whom traditionally the dowry represented the daughter's share of the parental property. In recent years there have been certain prevailing "market prices" for dowries. These vary with the education of the boy and his career prospects. A high school graduate might expect a dowry from his bride's family of around five hundred rupees while a boy returned from post-graduate training overseas and with prospects of a good job in government or business would probably expect more than five thousand rupees. Indeed some boys have paid for their education abroad with their dowries before really settling down to family life and a career. Some states have also recently passed new legislation regarding the age of marriage.

All of this legislation is aimed at making more possible the realization of the new values involved in the freedom to develop individual selfhood—especially for women, by giving them equal rights and protection under the law in the marriage and family situation. No doubt the legal undergirding of these possibilities will in the long run have a major influence on patterns and structures of marriage and family life, including an increasing understanding of these rights as reflecting accepted values. The acts already have speeded up the claims made on such values now that legal appeal to them is possible.

Christians feel that they have several moderately specific things to say to these changing patterns. They feel that they can point to a more than human undergirding of these values and their expression in society. That this is so seems to be more or less accepted by a surprisingly wide segment of Indian society, whence come periodic suggestions of admiration for Christian family life. Also, through intimate contact with the westernizing influence of the modern missionary movement, many Christians are from one to three generations ahead of the rest of India in attempting to live in modified patterns of marriage and family life. Because of this they have experience to share both about possibilities and about pitfalls. Throughout India this experience of Christians in modified patterns may be rather spotty but it does include experience based in most of the major subcultural backgrounds, including those associated with tribal, caste, and outcaste peoples.

The experience of ancient indigenous Christianity in the South is also of value, because, in accepting many of the new values during the recent generations of contact with Western Christianity, it has had to face up to the difficulty of their relevance to and impact on a traditional social structure little different from that of some of their Hindu neighbors. The kinds of changed patterns these Syrian Christians have experienced, coming without radical conversions, have been similar to those which most caste Hindus must attempt. In this effort the Christian experience has had some successes (including some preservation of the forms of marriage arrangement by elders while allowing for the possibility of some actual love matches within the traditional forms). Still, it is criticized by many Syrian students as being too slow to change and too tradition ridden, especially because of the dowry system. This may offer some guidance and some warning.

CITIFICATION

These family changes are an example and a harbinger of a citified style of living which has almost endless ramifications for India and for the Indian church. While it is in certain ways similar to the rather recent coming of urbanism as a way of life in America, it is different in more ways than it is similar. Citification has deep and far-reaching effects even in remote villages. This is partly because all village development plans are made by city-oriented officers, most of whom are actually themselves based and housed in the cities. Then too, in addition to the city-village communication effected by the government, commerce, and mass media, many village laborers and students are exposed to the city and bring elements of its life back with them to the villages.

Probably more than in the case of family life, the forces causing the citification of life are leading to changed social patterns without a thorough acceptance of new sets of values. This makes the changes doubly difficult for those who experience them, for those who study them, and for those who hope to do good through them. One important example of this is in the area of custom and law. Custom dictates almost all social behavior in the village. The laborer coming to the city from the village finds that most of the custom he knows is clearly irrelevant and that the rest is either forbidden or laughed at or both. He soon finds his life being directed by contract and other law, for the understanding or appreciation of which he often has little or no basis. This adds a queerness to the loneliness and disorientation in other ways that he usually feels initially even if he is fortunate enough to find a steady job. While those above him may not have exactly the same problems, they have similar ones of required social behavior rooted neither in custom nor in accepted, internalized, new values.

Often this value-rootlessness has bizarre effects, as in the fairly superficial example of a wealthy business family in one of the upper-class apartments on Marine Drive in Bombay, in which the elders, when they are alone, eat with their hands while seated on the floor in their customary way but insist that the grandchildren of the house, who eat earlier, be served seated at table with silver and china. The primary value involved seems to be only that sitting at table is coming to be the "done thing" in their social set. Often law for those in the process of citification is only the "enforced thing," and legal behavior is valued for no other reason. This again raises the whole question of the rule of law and its basis. Here it may be enough to reiterate that a change in patterns without accepted values to undergird this change creates an unstable and confusing condition.

While in the first instance citification involves a breakdown in traditional social structural bases of community as well as in the values and customs that supported them, it is clear that there are developing in Indian cities a number of new structures in which community may be, indeed must be, found. Some of these are on a geographical neighborhood basis but most are based more on some other kind of common interest. Probably the group involving the largest number of people is that of the labor unions and other organizations for laborers. The unions make up the predominant part of this group. In India, unions are frank adjuncts of political parties, and all the major parties have these adjuncts. This means that competition between unions in any particular plant reflects many wider political matters from outside the plant, and sometimes executive decisions are made locally in the light of wider political goals, rather than with primary attention to local industrial wants. While this may be seen hopefully as widening the view of the local community, in practice it has tended to discourage many workers, and perhaps especially Christian workers who are suspicious of the worldliness of politics, from active participation. In addition to union and political meetings and activities in which the members may participate, most unions have social halls with social education programs located near the plant or near the workers' homes. Some of these programs are for wives and children as well as for the workers themselves. Many plants also have company controlled welfare, educational, and social centers as a part of the labor welfare work that is required of them by law. All these aspects of union and labor welfare programs not only tend to transmit new values to the laborers and their families but also provide potential nuclei for voluntary associations, which seem to be a most promising basis for community in the city situation.

Other kinds of voluntary associations are growing in number and size among the city middle classes. Frequently these include a factor of social uplift, either for the membership group or for persons less well off than the members. These include regional language area associations, which help to preserve their special cultural heritage in distant cities, often through running schools. In the abstract these associations may seem divisive, and in some ways they are, but in this period of transition they are very real nuclei of community. There also are business and professional associations. Typical is the movement toward Rotary Clubs, and now toward Lions Clubs as well, in many cities. While in a sense these are as good and also as superficial as their counterparts in the States and Canada, yet for most members they offer the very first chance for full participation in voluntary associations crossing regional, caste, professional, and religious background, and may be seen as crucial in this trend. Religious voluntary associations are also rising in the cities. In addition to providing nuclei for community, all these kinds of voluntary associations also involve a priceless arena for gaining experience in free democratic

A typical example is a group of small landowners, all of whom kept cows. They formed themselves into a co-operative, with their own investment and a government loan, in order to buy the equipment needed to carry their pooled milk to a nearby large city every day. Here they sold the milk through a government-sponsored milk marketing scheme. These people took over two years to get their milk co-operative formed. Several of the young men in it had thought of it as a possibility but did not know how to go about getting it started. They sought the help of a local government official, who got them some information about the program of government aid through loans to co-operative societies. The elders in the village were very cautious about committing themselves to the proposed scheme. Some of them feared that the co-operative might somehow form a political base which would challenge their leadership and control. After the group interested in forming the co-operative had grown a bit, its members approached a missionary who was living a simple life of witness and service nearby. With his encouragement and finally with his help in filling out the forms and drafting their bylaws, the group grew large enough through slow persuasion to get the co-operative founded. The process of learning to work together, under simple parliamentary rules, which started when the group first came together, continues as the members manage this milk co-operative. This is the first formal voluntary association to be formed within this particular village. This example is also somewhat typical in that the primary benefactors are not from the lowest economic strata of the village. This too often seems to be the case although much effort is being devoted to development in the lower strata.

COMMUNITY AND *KOINONIA*

Co-operatives, an important center of voluntary associational activity and experience for their members, may become valuable nuclei for community.

Members of the left-wing Gandhian Sarvodaya movement and many other national leaders seek local and national community in a classless and casteless society. While this is true to much Gandhian thought and serves a real function as a dynamic for social change it seems to be much too idealistic since it does not speak of the positive structure of society. With increasing differentiation we might expect more classes. Certainly there is no difference in personal worth on account of class position. But—human nature being what it is—every society will probably have to reward some of its key people who perform difficult or distasteful tasks requiring either unusually hard work, long preparation, or special talent and ability, or all of these, more highly in money or status, if it considers the jobs they are doing to be important. With this basis, something like classes will arise. We would, however, advocate maximum opportunity for class mobility for all.

In regard to community, several contributions are offered from the Christian side. It seems clear that the neighbors of some city Christians do find that there is among them more of a feeling of mutual concern and friendship, without regard to regional or caste background, than is to be found in the profound isolation of many other families in the same neighborhood of differing caste and regional origin. No doubt this is often very imperfect among Christians. It was, however, so striking in one part of Delhi that a doctoral candidate who was making a social survey of the area has devoted a whole chapter of his thesis to it. He came to the situation with very little previous contact with Christianity, concerned only to describe what he found. He found that in general in this area geographical neighbors from different regional and caste backgrounds have almost no social intercourse at all while the Christians, alone among identifiable groups, visit and help each other without much regard to such backgrounds.

Early mission compounds, where converts from different castes came to live together in one community, also offered a clue to community that was lost as those mission compound Christians gradually became socially encapsulated and much like a Christian caste. The missionary-encouraged mass movements in some village areas also brought certain levels of openness for community between different caste groups which converted *en masse,* even though they would not always drink from the same cup in their service of Holy Communion or permit their children to intermarry. It seems to us that this is just where *koinonia* is relevant. No doubt *koinonia* is community in our Lord and, without him, is something less than full community. Nevertheless, it is also a revealed and ideal type of community, and we Christians feel compelled to take from it the best we know for the national search toward communities local, regional, and national. Our basic clues in this direction seem to be offered by the congregational life of the churches in India, as imperfect as this may often be.

However, beyond this we seem to see something that might be called "secular *koinonia*." Where a community of Christians, rooted in worship and motivated by the love of Christ, transcends the traditional segregation and group division and experiences a wider and fuller humanness in their mutual relations, they are able to help the whole neighborhood, including members of other religions and of no religion living around them, to share their vision of the human community cutting across rigid barriers. This is what we call "secular *koinonia*." This has been the experience in some Christian colleges, schools, and hospitals, in which many of the staff were non-Christian and yet in which there was a special sense of community, the reflection of Christian community, among the entire staff. This atmosphere of some church-related institutions has been admired by many Indian leaders. In short, this "secular *koinonia*" offers an example of community that may and does serve as a goal in the new India.

4 • THE SEARCH FOR NEW CULTURAL FOUNDATIONS

TRADITION AND CHANGE

We have dealt briefly with the trends and problems that India faces in building a new political and economic order as well as in setting new patterns of community. We have also indicated the revolution that these involve in the institutions and conceptions which characterized the traditional life of the people. Some of India's traditional institutions and conceptions are clearly no longer relevant to the living of life under new patterns, as in the following examples.

The Locus of Initiative

The development of personality in the joint family has stressed the suppression of open conflict within the group. Thus, little experience has been gained in the initiation of decision making, since this is the prerogative of the elder. This lack of experience in initiating decisions tends to undermine adult ability to make the many personal choices required both of citizens and officials in a democratic situation. The deferring of decisions to the elder, which has other cultural-religious roots as well, compounds this difficulty. Stories are all too common of responsible committee meetings in government, in political parties, and in churches where, under this cultural usage, young men with expert training or seething with ideas do not speak up. Dominance is in the hands of a minority of elders.

The Avoidance of Conflict

A related factor is that the cultural tradition tends to disvalue the open conflict of ideas and possibilities in favor of a consensus of social unanimity, usually enunciated by the elders. This is basic to Vinoba Bhave's version of democracy. It is, however, antithetical to the understanding of most democratic group procedure, in which the firm support of and interplay between different ideas seem basic. The same sort of avoidance of frank conflict is still found in many group elections. For instance, in the annual election of officers of a Y.M.C.A. managing committee, a prominent physician was nominated from the floor for the chairmanship. After some hesitation another name was also put forward. Upon this the physician, who undoubtedly would have been elected by a clear majority, withdrew. The facing of election conflict somehow didn't seem quite proper in this tradition. Distinguished political leaders have reacted in almost exactly the same way within party conventions. So, too, have student leaders in college and Student Christian Movement elections. Of course, this avoidance of open conflict does not mean that there is no pre-election activity to assure unanimity at the time of the election. Such "canvassing" by and on behalf of potential candidates is ordinary behavior. This canvassing takes on very great importance indeed when the elections themselves are more formal than in most democratic traditions.

The Third Man Role

Closely related is the high valuation that traditionally has been given to the "third man role" in Indian culture. This "third man" is the elder, *guru,* or sage who resolves conflict while standing above it. In democratic structures this means standing above, but also outside of, the real arena of responsibility. This was the natural role of Gandhi, who never assumed responsible office after independence. It is a role commonly sought by village elders and by political philosophers.

All these situations depend on certain basic traditional values. Some of these will be dealt with in later chapters. The rest of this chapter will attempt to outline some of the efforts that have been made to fill the vacuum caused by the discarding of traditional foundations found inappropriate in the face of newly accepted goals and values, with emphasis on the search for foundation in the arts, social philosophy, and religion.

THE CULTURAL RENASCENCE

The new life in India demands a new culture, a new ethos. Ferment is everywhere in the intellectual, artistic, and religious life of the country. India is in search of a new social philosophy adequate for the times, and for indigenous cultural incentives to sustain it in the face of the failure of the old values to meet new challenges.

In the past few generations this search has often led to attempts to revive ancient Indian arts and philosophies even though there may have been no living connection between present conditions and the atmosphere in which these once flourished. Most of the revivers were people exposed largely to European oriented education who were stimulated into attempting to bridge the gap they themselves felt between their westernized training and the Indian roots they sought. In Bengal, after an initial period of rejecting local modes and copying those of the contemporary West, artists began to imitate the Oriental style of Chinese and Japanese painting and then to copy the frescos at Ajanta in Western India, which are among the very finest in the world. In the same vein, pioneers in the church sought to become "indigenous" by taking on the coloration of ancient usage that was not really alive in the personal background of any of her members. Many students and others still worry about this gap. For instance, one who is becoming an excellent violinist feels slightly un-Indian about it because he plays Western music on a Western instrument. This seeking of roots in the past was also a seeking for nationality under colonialism and as such was a vehicle for nationalism.

Nevertheless, almost from the beginning of intercultural contact in Bengal there has been a genuine renascence going on, born out of a stimulation of genuine Indian tradition by new insights and possibilities. Tagore, the Nobel Prize winner, is typical of this, as is A. Coomaraswamy in his philosophy and interpretation of art history.

In the area of more directly political and social philosophy L. Tilak, R. C. Bal, Aurobindo Gosh, and others based militant nationalism on a frank revival of traditional Hindu festivals in order to promote unity and identity. They also used for this purpose an exposition and exaltation of the predominantly militaristic aspects of the *Gita,* the most popular Hindu religious scripture. Gandhi also sought roots for the freedom struggle and for the new nation in the Hindu tradition, and especially from within the *Gita,* but he interpreted its theme as a moral struggle of nonviolence. In this he went beyond the reforming revivalism of Tilak and the others, giving an entirely different meaning also to the terms *swaraj* and *swadeshi* which they had used, to form a new synthesis. Pandit Nehru has gone even farther in bringing humanistic thought into this synthesis. At the same time Nehru has frankly shucked off, for himself, the explicitly religious part of the tradition to the point where he seems to enjoy referring to himself as a pagan and sometimes goes out of his way when campaigning in areas near major historic religious shrines and places of pilgrimage to point out that although these have been the traditional holy places, for him the holy places in this new age are the dams, the multipurpose plans, the steel mills, and other sites of dramatic national development.

Since independence, such a continued renascence seems to offer the greatest hope for an adequate basis in combining the living elements in the tradition with the best of the newly accepted values. In a similar way it appears that the truly indigenous church will be that which relevantly speaks the word to contemporary reality in India in the midst of change. Out of such efforts an adequate spiritual basis may come, and it may come in some unexpected ways. Young professors of Indian philosophy and religion in at least four major Indian universities are seriously reading theologians like Bultmann and Tillich.

SECULARISM IN THE NEW CULTURE

The process of secularization is the major factor in the reorientation of culture in India. Secularization involves a differentiation between religion and the other aspects of society. This permits the liberation of the individual from the religious sanction of caste and collective authority. It also permits religious liberty, which is important to Christians, no doubt, but is also important to the full social utilization of the many persons of minority religious groups in India and keeps them all from becoming second-class citizens in some sense as they would be in, say, a Hindu state (or as we feel Christians and Hindus are in certain Muslim states).

This process of secularization also has dangers. These are already suggested by the search for new spiritual foundations, since it is precisely secularization that is responsible for the confusion of the human spirit. As Prime Minister Nehru has said, "The younger generation has no standards left, nothing to direct their thinking or control their actions." While this may not be altogether true, it does identify the danger. However, it is probably an inevitable danger in this kind of situation. The danger includes the possibility that this vacuum of instability may be filled by simple secularism, by militant religious orthodoxy, or by totalitarian communism.

In fact, there are numbers of instances in different parts of the country where many or all of these advantages and dangers are taking form in different segments of society in the same area. The typical example of this is where members of the upper-caste groups, on the basis of their better education, higher economic status, and longer exposure to the new values, move toward secularized "Westernization" in their manners, dress, taste, ways of doing business, and the merely routine observance or even the nonobservance of religious rites. At the same time a lower-caste group, which for reasons of low social and economic status has not until now been able to observe the more traditional values of religious observance and social propriety including vegetarianism, no divorce, and ban on widow remarriage, all of which the Westernized group has given up, may undergo a process of "Sanskritization" and begin to observe these and to hold other related values. Another group, still lower in the caste social scale, may renounce all the traditional values as having been used to keep them down, and find new life and hope and unity in breaking out into Buddhism or Communism or Christianity. In this last kind of group, in which radical conversion has taken place, we often find that radical factionalism, commonly noticed in village social groups when the traditional ways were threatened, has disappeared.

It should be observed that, while the process of secularization has both resulted in the present system of government and is in turn encouraged by it, the Indian Government is not precisely a secular state in the American pattern, that is, with a high barrier between state and religion. Neither could it be, because of the pattern left over from the British rule in which personal law is different for members of different religious traditions, and also because some vital steps for social freedom and democratization require coping with religious conditions and religious traditions. The conviction is growing in India that on *religious* grounds the state is neutral toward all religions, favoring none and discriminating against none. In practice, however, especially at lower levels, there is some fluctuation in policies at this point. Occasional favoritism is shown toward the majority religion, for example in incorporating its rites into government functions on the opening of buildings or in the observance of national holidays and in the enactment into law by some state legislatures of some of its cherished positions, such as an absolute ban on the slaughter of cows.

In general the fluctuations in the direction of secularization seem much more creative and dynamic than do those toward the orthodoxy of tradition.

On the other hand, there is for many leaders of political thought a fluctuation between secularism as a technique for political and social action in a religiously pluralistic society, and in secularism as a total faith. The latter secularism is an affirmation of the self-sufficiency of natural science, social science, and a correct understanding of human history to literally save mankind. As a total philosophy it either is indifferent to religious truth or denies it. A number of the major movements of social reconstruction in India, including much of the leadership of the Community Development Program, seem to be motivated by this philosophy, although they use religious traditions as a means of education. In the South the leaders of the *Dravida Kazhagam* and the *Dravida Munnetra Kazhagam* are dogmatically rationalist and militantly antireligious. In its protest against traditional religious sanctions and religion itself, the neo-Buddhist movement and its associated Republican Party are equally rationalistic. Nevertheless, even these radical movements perform a positive function in breaking down old barriers. They reflect and incite social dynamism.

TOTALITARIAN COMMUNISM

Marxist communism also has a large following and so represents an important part of India's search for new foundations. Many turn to it in despair or when the promises of others seem too long in coming. Essentially, however, since this position really dispenses with democratic humanism and individual freedom, it may be considered not so much a foundation for the new goals as a resort of persons frustrated in their attempts to reach those new goals.

RENASCENT HINDUISM

Sharply differentiated from secularism and communism is militant Hinduism, which calls for a Hindu state and a return to tradition and orthodoxy in social structure and religion. This position, equally with communism, dispenses with democracy and human freedom and offers a foundation for something other than present-day India. Many who feel their hereditary status threatened or who are merely feeling uncomfortable before the unknown threat of radical change are attracted, more or less, to this position.

Most thoughtful Hinduism, as opposed to the rather unthinking following of a tradition that is certainly the dominant mode, especially among the masses, may be characterized as renascent Hinduism. This renascence has many strains, but in general it stands for what has been called "the reintegration of the Indian culture in the light of modern knowledge and to suit our present day needs, and the resuscitation of its fundamental values in their pristine vigor."[1] While on the conservative side, this whole movement is generally most constructive. Much of it is based at least in part on the kind of thought best exemplified by the thinking of S. Radhakrishnan (who is now Presi-

---

[1] Notes will be found in the Appendix.

dent of India) or on that represented by the Ramakrishna Mission. But much is not. In general this thought is often muddled by the implicit assumption that Indian culture and Hinduism are somehow coterminal.

At a small consultation with Indian Christian theologians and scholars in 1961, some of the leading scholars of renascent Hinduism awoke to the fact of this implicit assumption and its falseness. At the close of the consultation, they admitted that for the first time they had come to realize that now Christianity was also really an *Indian* religion rather than a Western import.

It is not uncommon for Christians to be tempted in pride to accuse the teachers of renascent Hinduism of borrowing from or stealing from Christianity as they have reinterpreted classical Hindu positions in the light of the modern temper. This accusation both lacks charity and reveals an awfully confined theology about the possible activity of our Lord. Christians also frequently complain of some of the uncharitable interpretations of empirical Christianity made by older thinkers in this movement. But it appears to us that these thinkers were merely speaking in the only context of confrontation that they knew—a context that had been set by their missionary teachers in their negative proof texting from Hindu literature and traditional Hindu practice in order to show the superiority of Christianity.

In much renascent Hinduism there is a real concern for safeguarding human liberty, for recognizing many inherent rights of man, and for evolving an order of society which would promote responsible relations between men in a conscious sense of solidarity and justice. However, there is some question whether movements such as the Ramakrishna Mission and the Arya Samaj, which base their position in a modified Advaita, have really done full justice to human individuality, the urge for material progress, and purposive history.

The Sarvodaya movement founded by Gandhi and now under the leadership of Vinoba Bhave has been another and more consciously syncretistic force in reforming traditional Hindu culture and indigenizing the humanism of Western culture. Its emphasis on moral values gives purpose to human freedom and community. As a vigorous voluntary movement it seems to revitalize village community. But in certain forms the Sarvodaya movement does not seem relevant to a growing technical society, especially in urban areas. Because it does not seem to recognize evil in the spirit of man, the movement has undue optimism about achieving social justice through "heart change" and the practice of trusteeship. It is probably against this background that so much of the gossip overheard in trains, buses, and waiting rooms at the time of the last general election seemed to be arguing eventually that the "right type of man" in this office or that job was the *real* solution.

ACADEMIC IMPOTENCE AND POTENTIAL

Education is the means by which the clues to new foundations are being promulgated throughout the country. The absolute and proportionate increase in the numbers of those who are in school now over the position in 1947 is breathtaking. At the college level many schools are run by sectarian groups, but all are virtually supported by the government. This includes the Christian colleges. Even those related to boards and societies whose denominational officers take a very strict line in the United States on the use of government money by church-related institutions, in India get practically all of their regular budget from low tuition and government grants.

In no college does there seem to be an integrated presentation of potential new foundations. The sectarian schools, in so far as they make any such presentation, tend to color it to their own beliefs and background. Most students study to prepare for jobs; few other reasons exist. The system of external examinations, patterned on the older usage of London University, a revised form of which is described and damned by A. N. Whitehead in his *Aims of Education,* vastly reduces the instructors' initiative. It requires them to teach precisely and only what is prescribed by outlines made up by a committee of senior teachers of the university, on which they probably don't have membership, and with examinations on these outlines set by senior teachers of other universities whom they probably haven't even met. Nor does the heavy work load of the instructors, averaging twenty-two to twenty-three hours of lectures a week, encourage their initiative. If improvement of college education is to be achieved, probably a handful of excellent Christian and other private colleges must lead the way with help from the government. No other hope is apparent.

5 • WHAT IS GOD DOING IN INDIA?

This question arises from the theological assumptions with which we started. It has never been absent from our survey of India's struggle for a new selfhood in state, society, and culture. It was implicit in some of the deeper human and spiritual interpretations of the struggle which alone could give our survey some sort of coherence. In this chapter we propose to discuss explicitly the question: What is God doing in the Indian revolution we have surveyed?

Because of the universal Lordship of Christ, it is possible to affirm that God is in control of the world and is working out his purpose in the world. In the ultimate analysis this is an affirmation of faith and not of sight. This is a hidden Lordship. From this starting point some have gone further to ask whether it is not presumptuous for the faithful to seek to know the exact ways in which God is working in the world. His work remains a mystery, and those who have sought to unveil it and to know *how* God works in particular historical epochs and movements have usually ended in identifying the orders and movements that they consider good and in which they participate as the order of Creative Providence or the movement of Divine Redemption; they have become self-righteous themselves and have ended up playing Providence, that is to say, God, to history. The history of the church does show that over and over again she has fallen into this danger. So it is sometimes maintained that the only way to avoid this pitfall is to proclaim the gospel of the Cross, the Resurrection, and the Parousia, to confess the universal Lordship and never to seek to translate faith into sight.

Is it right, then, to speak of God's work in the revolution and run the risk of identifying attractive parts of it with the movement either of Creation or of Redemption? This problem is a most serious one. We are too prone to see the sinfulness of and divine judgment on the particular order that we oppose and to forget the sin in and divine judgment on the movement in which we participate. This, however, is not sufficient reason for refusing to seek to know just where God is creating, judging, and redeeming in our situation. Such refusal would permit Christians to become involved in the secular and religious movements of our time without the resources of *Christian* criteria. It would seem to mean either that Christians withdraw from such involvements (an obnoxious kind of pietism) or engage in them on the basis of philosophies unexamined in the light of Christ (a compartmentalization of personality). True theology is never a tool of self-justification but of judgment and redemption of the self. Even the missionary movement and the churches should be seen under the judgment and redemption of God. Our involvement in the world in obedience to faith demands that faith must seek to understand and discriminate between what God is doing as Creator, as Judge, and as Redeemer of the individual and of the world. Of course, we must always recognize that since we see now only through a glass darkly, the insights of our faith are never unambiguous.

It is dangerous to attempt to fit the history of salvation into the history of our time. But it is perhaps even more dangerous not to work out the implications of the faith that the kingdom of God and his Christ are present and active in the kingdoms of this world, and that the forces bringing the world to its consummation in Christ form the primary reality of our world. We would like to make our own the words of the 1959 Kuala Lumpur Assembly of the East Asia Christian Conference. It said:

> . . . it (the Christian gospel) is a gospel of the Kingship of Christ over the world. Therefore the meaning of world history, including that of modern Asian history is to be discovered in that Kingship which today is hidden and will be revealed at the end

> of time. The Church must endeavor to discern how Christ is at work in the revolution of contemporary Asia, releasing new creative forces, judging idolatry and false gods, leading peoples to a decision for or against Him and gathering to himself those who respond in faith to Him, in order to send them back into the world to be the witnesses to His Kingship. The Church must not only discern Christ in the changing life but be there in it, responding to him and making his presence and lordship known.[2]

With consciousness of the ambiguities involved in our task, let us look tentatively at what God is doing in relation to the Indian revolution today.

GOD AND THE FULLER LIFE OF MAN

Through the present revolution, God is offering to the people of India the vision of a fuller and richer human life and is creating the conditions necessary for its fulfillment.

What we speak of is not the utopianism of the religion of inevitable progress, which is not unusual in India, even inside the church, but which seems to us to be so untenable as to no longer require rebuttal. While we are reluctant to use the word "progress" because of its association with the religion of progress that dominated the interpretation of history in the recent past, we have been using expressions like "coming of age," "maturity," "entering into history," and "adulthood" of the masses in India. These terms indicate that growth at certain levels is discernible in the revolution of which we speak. The philosophers of progress went wrong in thinking that heaven is around the corner and in ignoring new evils and the possibility of regression. There is, however, a kind of progress possible in the conditions of humanness, which makes both hell and heaven nearer than ever before and which increases the acuteness of the conflict between them. It is in this sense that we can speak of the Indian revolution as offering the promise of Christ for a richer human fulfillment.

The growth in the conditions of a more fully responsible life can be discerned at various levels in the changes that are taking place in India.

Creativity

The Indian revolution contains within it man's search for freedom as the power and the responsibility to create. The increasing mastery of nature in science and industry as well as the creation of new dynamic forms of community in the place of old static social structures represent the new urge to exercise creativity which has been released. As has been said, there is a great deal of atheism and secularism in India. But part of it is a protest against those ideas of God and of the religious integration of society that would not give room for man's creativity.

Selfhood

Man's search for responsible selfhood is central in the ferment in India today. The revolution is marked by a new sense of self-awareness that is expressed in the demand for self-determination and self-development. The national struggle for freedom was a movement expressing the nation's self-awareness. In the process of nation-building all individuals and groups in India are being awakened to a similar sense of selfhood and its rights. This indicates the discovery of an essential element of man's humanness. Knowledge, on the part of the self, of itself and other selves also creates more problems of alienation and conflict than before. But alienation and reconciliation, hell and heaven, are meaningful terms and real possibilities only to those who know themselves to be responsible selves. This self-knowledge is undoubtedly an aspect of the growth of man's humanity.

Personality in Community

Through many changes, the people of India are seeking more humane forms of social justice and community than they ever knew before. They are rejecting traditional collectivism with its suppression of individuality and equality. What the outcastes—on the lowest rung of the traditional hierarchy—revolt against most is paternalism. It is felt to be inhuman because, while the whole system reduced persons to functions, it personalized the areas of life that ought to be treated impersonally in terms of law. For this reason even the anonymity and impersonality of an urban mass society is welcome to them as a resort and a protest. Of course, the search of the people is for a community transcending traditional collectives, atomic individualism, and industrial mass society, a community in which both law and love will be creatively related. This is a search, even when naive, for the social conditions of men's humanity. It is a search in which the church of Jesus Christ is vitally interested.

Purposive History

Through the revolution the Indian people have come to a greater sense of history as destiny. The worldview of resignation, the fatalism of the static patterns of living, and the cyclic conceptions of history are giving way to the dynamic of purposive history moving toward goals. The goals may be misconceived or even missed. This brings a tragic element into the picture. India never produced tragic plays because it knew no tragedy, but only fate. The new sense of historical purpose, even if it brings tragedy and despair, opens up a higher dimension of human existence for the people.

The Hell in the Midst of Hope

It is necessary to reiterate that the vision of heaven brings hell nearer. The revolution has brought into being also new spiritual powers of evil that may well emerge victorious. The spirit of individual and collective egoism, self-righteousness, and idolatry have acquired a new militancy and are likely to betray the promise of the fuller life in the revolution. About this, briefly looking again at the same four levels of growth toward humanness, we may say the following:

* Creativeness, newly found, may tempt man to elevate himself to the position of Creator.
* Self-discovery leads to self-centeredness, expressing itself in the self-seeking of man for power. This in turn results in new forms of exploitation and in the endless, frustrating

search for moral self-justification, which leads to ideological fanaticism.

* The revolution that seeks justice and community may lead to a new ruthless tyranny or to anarchy. It is always possible that men will replace the traditional impersonal collectivism with a depersonalizing sort of technical society.

* The sense of history and historical purpose and historical vocation may lead the nation, or some class or other group within it, to set itself up as a new Messiah to save mankind and bring history to fulfillment. This rather simple and utopian false messianism might well then be the precursor of totalitarianism and coercive tyranny, with or without a demagogue.

Looking at the Indian scene we see that all these evils are at work in the new society and culture that are emerging. The demoralization that the revolution has brought and may bring in its train has frightened many leaders and social reformers in the country. Some of them think that the evils of the old society were perhaps more tolerable. This feeling has given tremendous power to conservatism and the revival of old traditions. We must reiterate that there is nothing inevitable about the fulfillment of human aspirations, and there is a high degree of possibility that they may be betrayed from within. But the promise of Christ does not for this reason cease to be a fact. The answer to the new evils lies not in getting back to the uncreative, paternalistic, static patterns of the old collectivism, but in offering the victory of Christ over the powers of sin and death and of his New Humanity within the revolution and in releasing the forces that can redeem it from self-betrayal. Even so, we do not expect this victory to be complete within this or any revolution, nor are we quite sure that as victory it is exactly what we in our worldliness imagine.

GOD AND THE GOSPEL'S CHALLENGE

God is active in the Indian revolution preparing men and groups in India to face the challenge of the gospel of Jesus Christ.

Some of the pioneer educational missionaries of India like Duff and Miller, and even Macaulay, who as a civil servant played no small part in introducing the Western educational system in the country, thought that Western culture would reduce the hold of traditional religion on Indian people and prepare the way for their acceptance of the enlightened religion of Christianity. This hope has been belied, as K. M. Panikkar points out in his *Asia and Western Dominance*. There were some conversions to the Christian faith during the Bengal renascence among cultured Hindus who had received Western education, and the social ideas of Western culture did prepare the lower-caste groups for their group conversion to Christianity. But all these have virtually stopped, with Hinduism absorbing many social ideals and cultural values of Western culture and reviving itself in self-defense. When the Lindsay Commission on Christian Higher Education toured India, it found that what Western cultural impact had done was to drive Hinduism to a new self-consciousness and to introduce the new gods of nationalism and materialism from the West. It is therefore true that Western education and culture have not been a preparation for the gospel in the sense that they have led India more readily to accept Jesus Christ. In fact, the opposite seems to have happened.

When we speak of the Indian revolution as a preparation for the gospel, we are not saying that it will lead India to accept Jesus Christ, but rather that it will make the challenge of Jesus Christ clearer and more immediate. The revolution has awakened the people of India to certain new dimensions of personal and historical existence; this awakening makes the quest for a Christ almost inevitable. It may lead them to see that a choice for or against Jesus Christ has become largely inescapable. The revolution raises fundamental questions about freedom and responsibility, the human person and his destiny, the relation between law and love in community, the meaning of history in tragedy and fulfillment. In facing these questions most people must either accept Jesus Christ or become militantly anti-Christian in the depth of their spirits in the name of an ideology or religion that has the same structure as the Christian faith, with a scheme of redemption, a christ, a church, and an eschatological fulfillment. Yet there are also those who are neither hot nor cold. Some humanists, existentialists for instance, know much of Christ and his Church but neither affirm nor reject him. So too, there are increasingly many in India who in a characteristic Hindu way put the "Lord Jesus" on some sort of par with the many other lords whom they recognize. But ultimately the answer has to be Jesus Christ or a conscious rejection of him in the name of another messiah. The challenge to choose for or against Christ thus becomes clear.

In the Bible, all preparations for the coming of Christ have this characteristic: they have within them the potentiality of producing the anti-Christ. Israel was a preparation for the coming of Jesus Christ, but when he came Israel rejected and crucified him. God gave the law as a preparation for the gospel; it made clear man's alienation from God and his need of divine conciliation. But when Jesus Christ the reconciler came, the guardians of the law, the Pharisees, were most opposed to him.

The New Testament sees the appearance of the anti-Christ as a preparation for the coming again of the Christ. This is true not only at the end of history but also within history. For this reason the militantly anti-Christian forces within the Indian revolution, in so far as they are opposed not merely to Western culture but to the true core of the gospel (and to the church as the bearer of the gospel) must themselves be considered a potential preparation for Christ. The anti-Christ never remains the final answer—either in history or at the end of history.

GOD AND HIS WITNESSING PEOPLE

Through the modern Indian revolution God is judging and renewing his people to be a witness to his gospel in India.

We have referred to the church of Christ sojourning in India as God's chosen witness to his work in the Indian revolution. We must also point out his activity in gathering,

and culture, of self-righteousness, self-seeking, idolatry, and messianism by individuals and groups.

* Spiritual resistance to the spiritual idolatry and messianism within the revolution, in the name of Christ and his victory over principalities and powers.

* The demonstration of the power of Christian fellowship to transcend all barriers of class, creed, and ideology within itself and to be a power to break the rigidity of the same barriers outside of itself and thus to strengthen the idea and practice of an open human community in the nation.

In India today the church has the formal and real freedom for constructive participation in nation building, and for prophetic criticism of the institutions and ideologies that tend to bring disorder and to destroy the freedom and responsibility of men. The extent of this freedom varies from area to area. For instance, where Hindu communalism has greater hold, as in the central state of Madhya Pradesh, this freedom may be greatly limited, while in Bengal and Kerala, where Christians have a longer tradition of participation in cultural and political movements, their freedom is more real. The important question is whether the church has made use of this freedom creatively.

Spiritual resistance against the idolatrous spirit involved in most revolutionary and reactionary movements of our time is a continuous task that the church must perform. In a more or less open society, as in India today, this goes with constructive participation. Of course, it is possible that the situation in India might change so that the state, society, and culture would come under the control of a totalitarianism of the Right or of the Left. In such an event what spiritual resistance should mean is a question that would then have to be considered, but not until then. The present in India is, for Christians, no time for a simple martyr's heroism or for withdrawal from politics or for political resistance. Today in India the church's task is the more tortured and complex one of participating in the nation's struggle to define the goals and to exercise spiritual discrimination and resistance against idolatries.

We have pointed out how the Christian fellowship in local congregations and in Christian service institutions produces a certain openness and inclusiveness among the whole secular neighborhood. In fact there is no greater inclusiveness possible than that which is offered in and through Christ. In some sense not only the Christian fellowship of the church but also the secular fellowship of the neighborhood have their source here. Because of this they can contribute to one another and strengthen one another. The church in India has yet to think through the mutual relationship in Christ of these two interpenetrating fellowships. It must do so if it is to be more effective in strengthening the idea of the open secular community and in exercising the ministry of reconciliation at that level.

The Proclamation of the Good News

The church must bring the gospel of Jesus challengingly and relevantly to the people of India. This involves it in many responsibilities, including:

* That of taking more seriously than ever before the un-

finished task of bringing the gospel to every person in every group, whether in village or city, throughout India.

* The task of affirming its solidarity with the people of India as they seek to grapple with the spiritual crises and issues underlying their search for a more responsible personal and social existence. It is only in such common grappling that Christians can help their fellow Indians articulate their quest for a redeemer and the critical questions related to this quest. This is the preparation of the people for facing the challenge of Christ. The church must be engaged in this preparation.
* The responsibility of presenting Jesus Christ in relation to India's spiritual quest for a Christ. This is a quest that is articulated at many various levels in both secular and religious forms. This must include a relevant clarification of the scandal of the Cross, of the Resurrection, and the inescapable challenge to every man to make his choice for or against Jesus Christ.

The Church: Household of God

The church has the task of being the household of God, into which those who decide for Jesus Christ—from any sector of Indian life—can enter and feel at home and from which they can go out into the revolutionary world of politics, society, and culture to serve and to witness with the support of the Christian fellowship. This means, at least, new concern for the following:

* The unity of the churches in India. Apart from unity as essential to the church's being, it is also essential for very

practical reasons, for instance in order to enable the church to change its structures in a way suitable to independent India and to help strengthen its potential for evangelism in the country.

* The renewing of the structure of the church. It is necessary for the church to unburden itself from the weight of the "colonial" tradition of relations between Western and Indian churches, and between the church and Christian service institutions, and between the church and the traditional Indian social structure, so that the church may build new structures that may more readily respond to God's activity in the Indian revolution in new forms of witness, service, and fellowship.

* The renewal of the theology, ministries, and the inner spiritual life of the church, so that they may become means of helping the people of Jesus Christ in India to discern God's activity among the Indian people and to witness to it in their daily work and secular occupation in state, society, and culture.

THE CHURCH AS PEOPLE

The church in India is primarily a people acknowledging and witnessing to Jesus Christ as Lord and Savior of the world. Yet even so the boundary of this church, this people, is not infrequently fuzzy, for on the one hand the congregations include many who are born into them and who in the caste-structured society of India can be nothing else but "Christian" on account of their birth. And on the other hand there are many, not in the congregations, who in characteristic Hindu fashion quote the Bible and talk of and sometimes pray to "the Lord Jesus." Nevertheless, calling any or all of these the people of God or the people of the Christ does not in any sense mean that Christ works only through the church or through Christian people. Christ is using the secular and non-Christian forces for his purposes. But it is the church, the Christian people, who can most often best recognize Christ in the aspirations and events of our time. As we have said, this recognition is by faith and not by sight. However, this recognition by faith may be translated into secular insights, hopes, and power, which our secular and non-Christian partners may, at least in part, see and share as the truth about man's personal and social existence. In this way faith may correct false ideologies and contribute to the development of a realistic humanism. It is thus that our partnership with non-Christian people in the common struggle for the best possible secular conditions for human living may acquire a Christian dimension.

We Christians are a minority in India. But in so far as we recognize Christ in the Indian revolution and relate ourselves to him in it we shall cease to be minority-conscious and shall be concerned more with defending human rights, promoting social justice, and building structures of state and society that are conducive to greater fulfillment of human responsibility, in partnership with others. Then the only rights we shall ask for ourselves are the fundamental human rights necessary to bring the distinct contribution of our faith to the partnership.

It is this emphasis on solidarity with the revolution and partnership with people in the secular tasks of nation building that appears in the call to the churches of the First Assembly of the East Asia Christian Conference. The call speaks of what the new setting means to Christians.

> [It] means that Christian people must go into every part of the life of our peoples, into politics, into social and national service, into the world of art and culture, to *work in real partnership with non-Christians* and to be witnesses for Christ in all these realms. It means that every Christian must recognize that his primary service to God is the daily work he does *in the secular world.*[3]

Indeed, few Christian people may "go into" certain areas of national life with a sense of Christian call. But it must not be forgotten that already the Christian people are there in "every part of the life of our peoples" and working in "partnership with non-Christians." Probably they entered their jobs primarily as a means of making a living, with perhaps some motive also for national service. The need is to help them to see that they are the church called to witness to Christ in their spheres of secular life, to make their partnership with non-Christians "real," and to "recognize" their daily work as their "primary service to God." It is in this way that we can give meaning to the definition of the Church as the people of God in the world.

PEOPLE AND INSTITUTION

The Church is not essentially a human institution. Yet as the body of our Lord it is genuinely within the created order, in which it is in some sense a social institution. It is in just this sense—the point of its humanness—that the Church is most apt to succumb to temptation. But this is perhaps also where men may most clearly attempt to exercise responsibility toward the church.

For the most part, as a social institution, the church in India was founded in the denominational and congregational patterns brought by missionary founders, although there have constantly been lively minority attempts radically to modify these by seeking patterns nearer to ancient traditional Indian religious and social institutions and by seeking patterns that would enable the church more clearly to speak to the very different situation of India. Denominations as such, of course, have no real roots within India. The reasons for which they originally became differentiated in the West had usually become less pressing—or even theologically irrelevant—by the time they were founded and perpetuated in India. Actually the division in India is differentiated much more highly than in any particular Western nation because there is almost a different denomination descended from every different mission board and society. Thus, for instance, there are two Methodist Churches in many Indian states and cities, that which is descended from America and that which is descended directly from Britain. Also, in spite of a sort of over-all federal union of Reformed and Congregational groups in North India, there are still separate structures, church councils, or synods, for those descended from the Church of Scotland, from the Irish Presbyterian Church, from the Welsh Presbyterian Church, and from American churches. In spite of the recent union of some Presbyterians in America, churches, members, and church bodies of American Presbyterian descent are still identified as "U. P.s" or "A. P.s," that is, those descended from the mission of the United Presbyterian Church of North America and those descended from the American Presbyterian Mission, related to the Presbyterian Church in the U.S.A. Of more recent origin is a small group of "Split P.s" decended from the movement led by Carl McIntire. Even within the Anglican communion, there are those who identify themselves as "S.P.G. Christians" (Society for the Propagation of the Gospel) or "C.M.S. Christians" (Church Missionary Society). Others identify with the Bible Churchmen's Missionary Society or the mission of the Canadian province. Members of the first two groups especially, because they are more widespread, will sometimes inquire about the location of the nearest "S.P.G. Church" or "C.M.S. Church" even though there has never been more than a single branch of the Anglican Communion in India, the Church of India, Pakistan, Burma and Ceylon, which is still commonly called the Church of India.

These lines are, of course, perpetuated by the flow of money and personnel directly from the originating societies to the churches. The problems these rather artificial structures accentuate are minimized in a church that is really based in India on broad confessional lines, as the Church of South India is, and maximized in those few places where there is still a strong "mission" organization carrying on separately from, and often very paternalistically toward, the local "Indian church" that is the congregational fruit of the mission. The historic ties and continuing financial relationships continue to exert strong though often subtle influences. Some of these run counter to the movement for church union, which, in addition to being a theological imperative, seems the only sensible way for the radical minority to organize itself and which in at least some parts of the Church of South India has served as a locus of spiritual freedom, maturity, and church growth.

A significant difference in the structure of the church in India as compared with that in Canada and the United States may be seen in the relationships between the church and mission-founded institutions. These differences exist even though the church's handbook of polity may be almost identical with its North American counterpart. In India there is often a complex and complete interinvolvement of the church and institutions, such as schools and hospitals, that are a part of it and that are cared for by church courts and annual church governing bodies. Not a few congregations are dominated by that part of their membership which is employed in the running of a nearby school or hospital. This sometimes gives them such an institutional stake in each other that it is difficult if not impossible to sort out all the lines of influence and involvement. Probably this is the way it must be. Certainly this relationship helps to keep the institutions from becoming excessively ingrown and isolated from the total mission of the church.

One curious outcome of this situation is that often on both the local and regional levels the leading laymen in a denomination are in fact officials, principals, or superintendents of the church-related institutions. On such councils they are no doubt strongly tempted to consider the well-being of the institutional life of the church rather than really being able to represent the true laymen of this situation—those whose occupations are really and completely in the world independent of church institutions.

Most foreign missionaries over the years have tended to enforce the discarding of traditional Indian forms of organization by new converts. So too the discarding rather than the "baptism" of all religious practices and most traditional cultural practices, all of which might have some religious base in the history of Hindu society, has been encouraged by many missionaries and new converts. This has not all been a matter of sneering at or being "petty-moralistic" about such traditional forms and practices. An additional factor in the situation seems to have been a real and sympathetic understanding of the temptations and pressures on the new converts to completely revert to their former styles of life, which were still all about them. This led to the putting upon them of especially hard demands of completely breaking away as a kind of special ethics for the missionary situation. Later generations may then go back and reclaim the good and redeemable in the culture.

For instance, in northeast India, where Christians have come from tribal backgrounds and where over one-sixth of all Protestant Christians in India live, the present generation of pastors, who are about third-generation Christians, are eagerly finding a place for tribal dancing, music, and art in church festivals. Indeed the churches may soon be the primary, and eventually the sole, centers preserving many aspects of tribal culture. But these things were totally rejected by the first generation of pastors because of their association with headhunting, tribal deities, and other practice incompatible with the gospel. Early anthropologists were very critical of the church in the first generation for deculturizing the tribal people. Now the older generation in the church is critical of the younger generation for permitting a return to tribal practices. Probably both generations have been essentially right for their own time in this matter. This discarding of cultural forms did not apply to family structure when families converted en masse. In fact much caste identification was carried over into the church and, as already noted, even after several generations Christians, especially from the mass movement areas, tend to marry only Christians with the same caste background. In much of the country, too, these Christians still retain special social ties with non-Christians of their former caste. This has provided a basis for understanding and penetrating society that may prove invaluable in years to come.

While the caste structure of society has affected the church by providing lines of family and influence that may be divisive in some areas, it has had another, more positive effect as well. This is evident in some mass movement areas where the traditional caste brotherhood organization, called *baradri* in the North, was not stamped out on conversion. Traditionally the *baradri* enforced morality and custom in the caste by carrying out social sanctions decided upon by a council of elders. In a few places this organization is so strong in the church that it still handles all such matters of morality and discipline. In these places litigation in church courts is pretty much reserved for formal institutional difficulties alone. Even where this is so, the *baradri* is a sort of "shadow" church court in that it has never been formally recognized. In its very liveliness and lay nature, however, it represents the taking up of true congregational responsibility in places where it functions.

We have also noticed above that the pervasive caste nature of traditional society has caused all Christians virtually to be encapsulated as a caste. This encourages the formation of Christian social ghettos. Further, it means that most evangelical groups have guilt feelings about the increasing numbers who are "Christians" simply because they were born of Christian parents: persons who are Christians by social definition alone, since socially they can be nothing else, without any reference at all to their religious experience. This situation is not unlike that of the half-way covenant situations that developed in some of the early American colonies that had sectarian bases. It creates an institutional pressure, upon those who are born into the Christian community, to "act like Christians," which on the whole is probably a good thing but which does compound the threat of legalistic moralism and petty-moralism that all churches face. The temptation of this threat is aggravated in India because it is in line with many ethical assumptions of the prevailing culture of popular Hinduism.

This enforced identification of Christians as a larger caste group has positive institutional characteristics. One speaks, idiomatically, about "the Christian folk" or "the Christian people." Some of the terms for this are *log* or *lok* meaning "folk" and *qaum* meaning "people" or "nation." These terms are widely used of Christians by non-Christians and by village Christians of themselves. This denotes *all* Christians in an area without regard to their denomination. It represents both a unity enforced from outside and a unity felt from inside as similar challenges are faced in a similar way. While not recognized by the churches, there have been efforts by laymen to organize this common Christian group for social purposes and for the exertion of political pressure. This unity is about as far as possible from the "spiritual unity" that is often insistently sought first, before permitting discussion of any other unity, by the opponents of church union schemes, but there is a sense in which it seems to be an overlooked gracious structure of actual union.

Historically Indian Christians come from three types of background: mission compound, mass movement, and ancient Eastern churches.

In the mission compound converts from various backgrounds, usually rejected by their families and caste fellows, found shelter, work, and a new community under the shadow of the institutional church. This usually meant forsaking their traditional way of life for a different way introduced by the missionaries.

Mass movements brought converts in rather large, not too well instructed groups into the church, each group comprising at least several larger families of the same subcaste from one village or from several adjoining villages. They stayed in their villages and usually in their traditional occupations, at least initially. Often there was little break with basic social structure or custom, which was carried into the church with some changes. Eventually paid "workers" or "evangelists" were usually given formal charge of these village congregations.

From Eastern churches come the Syrian Christians, who trace themselves back in tradition to the visit of St. Thomas the Apostle to India. Until their rather recent contact with Christianity from the West, their situation has been largely one of attempting to keep intact the traditional communal structure that encapsulated their separate identity through many generations.

None of these structures of the Christian folk seems really relevant to participation in the Indian revolution today.

PRESSING INSTITUTIONAL QUESTIONS

The Professional Village Evangelist

On the basis of thoughtful assessment by many, and some experience in the Diocese of Madurai and Ramnad of the Church of South India, the conviction is growing that the church must be freed of the professional village evangelist if there is to be a spontaneous expansion of the gospel by neighborly concern and enthusiasm from village to village. Experiments with the new patterns in areas without such evangelists have been exciting in their results. In the experiment in Madurai the first three Honorary Presbyters have now been ordained after a few weeks of training annually for the last few years. They continue in their old occupations in their villages, one as a farmer and another as a musician, and also serve their congregations as fully ordained presbyters. Those selected were already leaders and elders of their congregations. Their annual period of training will continue throughout the foreseeable future. While really basing the church on the natural village congregational group, this pattern also does away with the major economic problems of support for a full-time professional ministry as introduced from the West. Attempts radically to change the pattern where such paid evangelists exist have been less heartening.

Language and Indigenous Religious Expression

The day to day life of the churches may not differ so much from that of churches elsewhere as one would expect. The orders and forms of worship that have been handed down along denominational lines are too little changed. They are usually in the regional language, sometimes in a peculiar version of it which in one region is called missionary Tamil and in another missionary Hindi. But this is being outgrown—especially where different traditions are coming together. There has been a liturgical revival in parts of the Church of South India and in parts of the Syrian churches. In most cities the elite attend English language services. Recently the principal of a Christian college, in a group where each member was identifying himself and his congregation, slipped and said that he was from "———, the English church with the Christian language." No doubt many go to similar churches because of the social status involved.

Most major holy days are celebrated more thoroughly in India than in America. Good Friday continues to be a legal holiday for all government employees who are Christian. Even New Year's day becomes a major Christian festival. All festivals, including regular Sunday worship, have many more children involved in them or sitting around the fringes than would be seen in similar circumstances in America.

The Hierarchy and Financial Power

The professional ministry, especially in the cities, is very well trained. Usually the minister is one of the best educated men in the congregation; he is often one of the few well educated men there. This tends to set him a bit apart in prestige and power. Usually there is a district minister of some sort above him. While the salary of the city pastor will be supplied by the congregation, money for the support of the hierarchy above him and for projects such as new buildings and scholarships for Christian youth will come largely from abroad and will be administered by the hierarchy. This means that in India the hierarchy generally wields both spiritual and financial power. This is unlike the situation in American churches, where the financial power usually rests largely with the laity and almost wholly with the local church. Thus financial power which in North America is a countervailing power is in India likely to be a reinforcing power.

The Extension of Campus Ministries

The Student Christian Movement of India has been the church at work in the colleges for many years. It has led many into ministerial vocations and many more into a Christian understanding of their lay vocations. It has in many ways been the fertile ground for movements toward unity and liveliness, from the ashrams of recent generations to the Christian concern for the study of religion and society which is emerging in this generation. Before independence most of its work was done in the Christian colleges and a few university centers. Since that time the amazing multiplication of colleges and universities has forced it to expand at a very rapid rate in an effort to meet the growing needs of students in all of these places. This is because Christian students do not only go to Christian colleges. Usually there are no Christian technical colleges. Often it is cheaper or otherwise desirable for students to live as near home as possible. Sometimes it is impossible to get admission to a Christian college because there are many more applicants than there is room for. In a few places colleges other than Christian colleges may be sought because their academic reputations are better. In a typical large city about half of the Christian students may be in the one or two Christian colleges and the rest may be spread among a medical college, several science and engineering colleges, several law and teacher training colleges, one older government or private college of excellent reputation, and several newer colleges of lesser reputation. The S.C.M. feels some responsibility toward all of these students and also for maintaining a Christian presence in their colleges.

Competition Among Christian Groups.

During recent years the S.C.M. has had to contend not only with the urgency of expansion but also with the increasingly overt competition of the Evangelical Union, which is related to the Inter-Varsity Christian Fellowship. Some Christian colleges have periodically found it impossible to hold college chapel services because of the intensity of this competition. In one such institution the staff and students related to the Evangelical Union stopped coming to chapel services led by persons associated with the S.C.M. Then, when it was finally arranged that the two groups would alternate in taking responsibility for the services, a pentecostal movement boycotted all chapel services. This kind of fragmentation is much more noticeable in a Christian college in India, with probably no more than 15 per cent of its student body Christian, than it might be in America. It is often suggested that money and status provided from related groups overseas tend to encourage and maintain such fragmentation. Talks aimed at reconciling these two groups within the church have so far failed.

Nor is this the only evidence of disruptive sectarian activity. Most pastors in India complain of those who find it easier to count stolen members for their statistics, sent in support of appeals for more funds from abroad, than really to work for converts from outside the Christian community. Indeed, not a few leaders in the S.C.M. National Christian

Council group feel that surely God must somehow be working through the Government of India as it radically limits the number of new foreign missionaries who are granted visas, for many of us see that if it were not for this limitation there would by now be many thousands of dollar-financed sectarian centers of discord rather than the few hundred that do exist.

THE CHURCH AS ECUMENICAL FELLOWSHIP

On the more redemptive side of this same situation, it seems to us, the Indian church both as people and institution has to see itself as manifesting a reality that is essentially universal in character. It is always easy for the church to become the "image" of the world in which it lives. The nineteenth century missionary movement in India is being criticized today as having been too much identified with British power and British cultural penetration into India; in our time the temptation is for the church to become identified with the Indian revolution. The church's identification should be with God and not with the revolution, not even with the good and valuable part in it. The Indian church can maintain the transcendence of its being only if it holds to the universality of the gospel and the Church. At the same time, the church in India must maintain those relationships within the Christian world mission that help to give form to the concept of universality.

The Indian church should increasingly send its missionaries to preach Christ to people in lands other than India and maintain a partnership with the churches in these lands for this purpose. Parts of the Church of South India have had missionaries overseas for many years. This work is now concentrated in Thailand. The Methodist Church of Southern Asia has a missionary couple working in the church in Sarawak along with other Methodists from America and East Asia. The United Church of Northern India supports and provides staff for a mission undertaking in East Africa. All of the major denominations in India, along with many western missionary societies, work together in the United Mission to Nepal, which has been a joint venture since the initiation of permitted Christian service in medicine and education less than a decade ago.

The Indian church should be able to receive missionaries and other kinds of aid from churches of other lands for its task of evangelism and service in India. In general, in spite of certain regulations of the Government of India, the churches have the freedom to do this. These government regulations are not in any way anti-Christian, although cases may occasionally arise of government officers at the district level interpreting them as if they were. One facet of the regulations represents an effort by the government to assure that jobs are filled by Indians where there are qualified Indians to fill the jobs. Commercial firms under European management have been given rigid timetables and percentages for the filling of senior executive positions by Indians. With religious institutions the government is not so rigid and legalistic but the intent is the same. Surely this can only be good for the health of the church in India.

The other major facet of the regulations reflects the concern of the government for preventing any kind of intercommunal strife. The Hindu-Muslim slaughter at the time of partition and occasional small outbursts of the same feelings since then have frightened everyone. Foreign street-preachers and evangelists grossly condemning other religions in favor of Christianity might lead to similar outbursts. Hence some types of missionaries are not permitted to enter India. This too may contribute to the health of the church by leaving more scope for a really Indian approach to evangelism, by emphasizing the preaching of the gospel rather than the sometimes overly egocentric "saving of souls," and by reducing potential foci of Christian factionalism and "sheep-stealing."

Both the sending and receiving should be set within the framework of the mutuality of an ecumenical community, expressing a common concern for God's activity for mankind as a whole.

Exactly what this means for the American churches and their relationship to the Indian churches has still to be worked out, not as an exercise in adjustment to the compulsions of nationalism, theological or educational fads, or missionary statesmanship, but in terms of their tasks of witness to the peoples of America and India.

APPENDIX

FOR FURTHER READING

Appasamy, A. J. (ed.), *Temple Bells*. Calcutta: Association Press, 1930. An example of the search of Bishop Appasamy and a group in South India to find Indian roots for the gospel and the church.

Campbell, Ernest Y., *The Church in the Punjab*. One of the most discerning of the I.M.C. Study Series on the churches in India. The rest of the series is listed in it.

Devanandan, P. D. and M. M. Thomas (eds.), *Christian Participation in Nation-Building*. Bangalore: Christian Institute for the Study of Religion and Society, 1960. A summary of the Christian study of rapid social change in India, this book also contains a bibliography of that study and of the related publications of the Committee for Literature on Social Concerns and of the Christian Institute for the Study of Religion and Society.

Grant, John Webster, *God's People in India.* Toronto: Ryerson Press, 1959. The most perceptive book by any recent sabbatical year visitor. Presents with almost journalistic ease insights typical of a group of intellectuals within the churches.

Jhabvala, R. Prawer, *To Whom She Will.* London: George Allen and Unwin, 1955 (also published as *Amrita.* New York: W. W. Norton and Company, New York, 1955). This and Mrs. Jhabvala's later novels portray the urban family and personal aspects of the revolution with much authenticity.

Journal of American Folklore, Vol. 71, No. 281 (July-Sept., 1958). A good introduction to its theme of "Traditional India: Structure and Change."

Newbigin, Lesslie, *The Household of God.* New York: Friendship Press, 1954. Bishop Newbigin is the ablest active Protestant theologian writing from within the Indian church. An Indian flavor is found in all his works, but this one is most relevant to our immediate area of concern.

Panikkar, K. M., *Asia and Western Dominance.* New York: John Day Co., 1954. This is especially useful for a pointed and antagonistic analysis of the political and social aspects of the influence of the Christian missionary movement on Indian society.

Presler, Henry H. (ed.), *Student Research Monograph Series.* Jabalpur: Department of Organized Research of the Leonard Theological College, 1952, ff. No. 7, *The Industrial Parish,* by Nirmal Minz is especially good. This department is specializing in a mid-India urban situation. We look forward to some larger work from the hand of Prof. Presler.

Ward, Barbara, *India and the West.* London: Hamish Hamilton,

1961. By perhaps the best Western interpreter of India to the West, this book has been brought out in a cheap edition by the Government of India.

Wiser, W. H., *Behind Mud Walls in India.* London: George Allen and Unwin, 1934. A classic, still containing clues for the church that might be followed with profit. Also a key to Dr. Wiser's more technical work as the pioneer missionary social scientist in North India. We anticipate that a revised edition will soon be published.

SOME STATISTICS

In area India is almost half the size of the United States and hence about the size of Europe less the U.S.S.R.

As to religion about 85 per cent of the people consider themselves Hindu. Almost 10 per cent are Muslim, slightly more than 2 per cent Christian, and slightly less than 2 per cent Sikh. No other religious group is more than ½ per cent of the population. By way of comparison, Christians make up about ½ per cent of the population of Japan.

There are about 1300 colleges in India, divided among some forty-six universities. All degrees are granted by the universities. At the time of independence in 1947 there were only about seventeen universities, proportionately fewer colleges, and the size of the typical college was considerably smaller than today.

The following figures are approximations that reflect the general health situation:

	1947	1958
General death rate per 1000 population	19.7	8.8
Infant mortality per 1000 live births	146	92
Incidence of deaths per 1000 on account of:		
Fevers (esp. malaria)	10.8	3.6
Smallpox	0.1	0.31
Plague	0.3	0.0
Cholera	0.4	0.08

Dysentery and diarrhea	0.8	0.45
Respiratory diseases (incl. TB)	1.5	0.90

The National Malaria Control Programme was launched in 1953 with the assistance of the U.S. Technical Cooperation Mission and the World Health Organization. The proportion of clinical malaria cases treated in hospitals and dispensaries to cases treated for all diseases fell from 10.8 per cent in 1953-54 to 1.3 in 1960-61 and 0.6 by the end of September 1961.

There are thirteen major languages, in addition to English, recognized by the Indian constitution. Of these, Hindi or languages very closely related to Hindi form the mother tongue of about 45 per cent of the population, and at least another 20 per cent of the population have mother tongues related to Hindi. However, some of these latter, such as Bengali and Marathi, have richer literary traditions than Hindi, and this, combined with the linguistic basis of regionalism, does not make those who speak them very sympathetic to Hindi. Since independence English and Hindi have been the official languages of the central government. Hindi has been declared the national language, but it has been promised that the change-over at the center will continue to be slow and that there will be no "imposition" of Hindi on the non-Hindi speakers.

In 1961 the literacy percentage was about 24. In 1951, when the literacy rate was 16.6 per cent, with a total number of 60 million literates, only 3,800,000 were literate in English. As literacy increases, improvement will be most rapid in regional languages, next in Hindi, and least rapid in English.

English is still favored by many of the wisest leaders for purposes of technical education for the time being and as "a window on the world." In fact, at present English is *the* language used of necessity in most national and interregional meetings, whether called by the government or by the churches. English in this way is very much the common language of the intellectuals just as Latin was in Europe in the Middle Ages. No doubt it will die out in the same way too. We can hope that the church in India is not stuck with being its pallbearer as the Roman church has been with Latin.

SOME TERMS

Advaita. Literally "nondualism." The strongest of the so-called Vedantic schools of Hindu philosophy and philosophical theology. Always essentially monistic, but often with extreme subtlety and sophistication. Indian Christian theologians are tending to take it much more seriously than they once did.

Caste. A caste is an hereditary group bound together by exclusive intermarriage, interdining, and similarity of vocation. Each caste or subcaste has its own subculture and rather fixed social status within any given locality.

About 20 per cent of the total population has been in "outcaste" groups that rank at the very bottom of the social hierarchy. This whole bottom group has been considered religiously polluting and has been traditionally confined to very menial and crude jobs. Because of this members of such castes, along with the tribal people, have been considered so backward as to merit special concern in educational and vocational aid and uplift programs. These groups have been listed in a schedule appended to the Indian Constitution and hence are now commonly called "scheduled castes" and "scheduled tribes." Gandhi called them *harijans,* which he translated "children of God" in an effort to remove some of the traditional stigma from them.

Communal. A community in this sense is first a subcaste or caste and finally the whole group of coreligionists, Hindu, Muslim, or Christian. It is a group that looks to the protection and welfare of its own, often at the expense of other communities. Therefore it implies a large amount of group selfishness on the basis of hereditary groups, each somewhat different in traditional culture and status from the others. Such communities may become political entities that vote as a block to preserve or increase their common and often selfish interests.

Community Development. This is planned intensive social-economic uplift within a geographic area. The community here is the larger neighborhood.

Cottage Industries. These involve production by the larger family units, organized for resources and marketing with other families in the neighborhood. Often some traditional craft is implied but this need not be so. Subsidies are often given to such industries—this is especially true in the realm of cloth weaving on hand looms.

Dravida Kazhagam and *Dravida Munnetra Kazhagam.* Movements in South India accentuating the myth, based on historical facts, that the Dravidians were pushed into the south and exploited by the early Aryan invaders of India. The D.M.K. has become a potent cultural-political movement or revolt against Brahman domination. It seeks to purify (de-Sanskritize) the Dravidian languages and cultures of South India. In rejecting the Hindu religion, as a device of Brahman domination, it tends to reject all religion. A radical wing calls for a separate Dravidian nation outside of the Indian Union.

Gita. Short for *Bhagavad-Gita,* the Song of the Blessed One. This is a part of the *Mahabharata* and is the most popular of the Hindu scriptures. Because of its late place in the Hindu canon and because of its religious popularity, it is often considered the "new testament" of the Hindus.

Joint Family. The traditionally ideal form for family living in India. Involves the living together in one house with one hearth of most members of a family of considerable depth of generations. Such a family might include an elderly couple along with the man's parents, widowed sisters, younger brothers and their families, sons and their families, and unmarried daughters; they would have a common purse and common discipline.

Lok Sabha. The lower house of the Indian Parliament, corresponding almost exactly to the British House of Commons.

Neo-Buddhism. A movement made up by those of scheduled caste background who followed Ambedkar into Buddhism while renouncing Hinduism. Maharastra is the center of this movement.

Panchayatiraj. Rule by *panchayat,* the traditional ruling group of five elders in a village, caste brotherhood, or any other association. Now revived on a constitutional basis as a vehicle for decentralizing democratic rule. The elected local body has some real but limited economic, executive, and judicial powers. In this sense *panchayatiraj* is a very new introduction into a scene where there has not before been this kind of democratic responsibility at the local level.

Rajya Sabha. The upper house of the Indian Parliament.

Sarvodaya Movement. The whole complex of Gandhian uplift and self-help movements. The movement led by Vinoba Bhave and others, which might be called left-wing Gandhianism, stresses the co-operative use of land by villages relatively autonomous both economically and politically and assumes the need for and desirability of only a rather weak central state.

Social Worker. This has become a technical term for those who do rather paternalistic social uplift work. Most such social workers are members of the upper economic and social classes or general government officials. Not infrequently in the last decade official and unofficial commissions and committees have asserted that the ideal social worker must have a "missionary spirit," meaning a dedication to and concern for the people, such as early Christian missionaries had in the face of some hardship. Professional social work, a slightly different thing, has made great strides in training, practice, and acceptance in the last twelve years.

Swaraj and Swadeshi. "Home rule and home-made." The slogan of the later Indian independence movement calling for national self-government and internal economic development.

Zamindar. A large landowner, whose ancestors would have been tax agents rather than landlords. The local representative of a feudal system of landholding. Zamindari abolition does away with this and is intended to vest the land in the farmer.

NOTES

1. From the objectives of the Bharatiya Vidya Bhavan, an educational institution in Bombay under the leadership of K. M. Munshi.

2. U Kyaw Than (ed.), *Witnesses Together:* Report of the Inaugural Assembly of the East Asia Christian Conference (Rangoon, Burma: East Asia Christian Conference, 1959) p. 60.

3. *Ibid.*, p. vi, (italics added).

TEXT: LINOTYPE CALEDONIA 10/13 • DISPLAY: WEISS ROMAN
MANUFACTURE: SOWERS PRINTING COMPANY, LEBANON, PA.
DESIGN: LOUISE E. JEFFERSON